POWER UP!

LINKS

EDITION

POWER UP!
LINKS
EDITION

DEVOTIONAL THOUGHTS FOR GOLFERS

DAVE BRANON, EDITOR

Discovery House.

© 2009 by Discovery House
All rights reserved.

Discovery House is affiliated with Our Daily Bread Ministries,
Grand Rapids, Michigan.

Requests for permission to quote from this book should be directed to:
Permissions Department, Discovery House, P.O. Box 3566,
Grand Rapids, MI 49501.

Unless otherwise indicated, all Scripture quotations are from the
Holy Bible, New International Version®. NIV®. Copyright ©1973, 1978, 1984
by Biblica, Inc. Used by permission of Zondervan.
All rights reserved worldwide. www.zondervan.com

Interior design by Sherri L. Hoffman

ISBN: 978-1-62707-419-3

Printed in the United States of America

First printing of paperback edition in 2015

CONTENTS

INTRODUCTION

What is more basic than hitting something with a stick? What little boy or little girl, while walking through the woods, doesn't reach down, grab a tree branch lying on the ground, and proceed to swing it at anything that looks like a good target?

It's a simple, mildly entertaining action.

But if you take that stick, turn it into titanium, put a club face at the end, and use it to thwack a dimpled ball 200 yards or 20 feet (depending on your lie), that simple, mildly entertaining action turns into a gazillion-dollar sport that has captured millions of people.

People who love to hit something with a stick.

Surely the bug has bitten you, or you wouldn't be holding this book in your rubberized-grip-calloused hands. Surely you have a bag full of sticks in your garage, waiting to be tossed in the trunk so you can head off to your favorite links. Surely you wish you were hitting a Titlest with one of those sticks instead of reading this book—or maybe instead of doing much of anything else.

That's what happens when the bug hits—when the stick-swinging bug sinks its teeth into you and you find yourself watching the Golf Channel at 11:30 at night. Or you discover that instead of checking insurance or stock or inventory or medical statistics on the Internet during the work day, you are checking to see who is leading the PGA money list this week. Or you watch the eight-day forecast on your local TV channel just so you'll know which of those eight days will be good for stick-swinging.

Golf, it seems, is one of the most addictive activities known to humankind.

Think of some of the reasons why this is so:

1. You are out on God's green earth, soaking in vitamin D-laced sun rays and actually doing exercise. It's a perfect storm of goodness: Recognizing God's creative work while doing your body some good.

2. It's a challenge in every swing. Each time you line up your golf club to smack that ornery little ball into submission, you are demonstrating to anybody watching that you have hand-eye coordination, strength, wisdom, calmness, good vision, and athletic ability (or not). It is just you and the course—and no one to blame but yourself if you send the ball into a watery grave or into solid contact with a hundred-year-old oak tree.

3. This is a social activity. This isn't basketball, where you use up all your energy just getting up and down the court, and you don't have any breath left to use for words—and nobody wants to talk anyway because they're all gasping for breath. In golf, you stroll. You stop. You contemplate. You hover over the ball. You have more than enough time to talk, to explain, to make excuses, to test your ability to use acceptable words when bad things happen.

This book is for stick-swinging people. It is a chance for you, stick-swinger, to sit down in your favorite chair and know that even though you are not playing golf at that very moment, you are at least reading about it. You are reading articles by people who play golf for a living (is there a more blessed job on earth?) or who do other things to earn their bread but who have some interesting golf stories to tell you. Think of it as a golf substitute.

And as you read, you will gain important insights that can make you a better person, a more godly human, and a more focused worker, spouse, or parent. Sorry, we can't make you a better golfer, but who knows, those good things this book does for you just might improve your game overall (hey, it's worth a shot).

So sit back, pull on your favorite golf shirt, turn the Golf Channel on for background, even wear your golf shoes if it makes you feel better—and dig into *Power Up! Links Edition*.

It's the next best thing to hitting something with a stick.

—DAVE BRANON, EDITOR

THE TOP 100 GOLF COURSES
IN THE UNITED STATES

*A*rt Stricklin has spent a major part of his adult life hanging *around some of the top golf courses in the United States. Award-winning Dallas-based golf writer Stricklin has visited those courses in search of information for the hundreds of articles he has written on golf over the years. His work has appeared in* Texas Monthly, Sports Illustrated, Sports Spectrum, *the British Open program,* Augusta National Golf Club publications, *and even the* Peoples Workers Daily *in China. Stricklin has written seven books, including the* Texas Golf Guide *and* Links, Lore, and Legends: The Story of Texas Golf. *So, it was a natural choice to choose him to pick the Top 100 Golf Courses in the United States. Just so you know, Stricklin has what he calls "a shaky 14 handicap," but he has nailed a hole-in-one.*

The rankings for The Top 100 Golf Courses in the United States were taken from a mixture of golf history, prestige, and public access. One of the great things about the game of golf is that everyday players can play the same course with almost the same conditions as their professional golfing heroes. It's a unique charm of the sport that can be seen nowhere else. Try playing a softball game at Fenway Park or a touch football game at the Rose Bowl. That's a large part of the reason why courses like Pebble Beach, Bandon, Pacific Dunes, and Pinehurst are ranked so highly.

Another lure of golf is the great history and tradition associated with the sport. That is what raises up courses like Augusta National, annual springtime home of the Masters golf tournament, along with Winged Foot, Shinnecock, and Pine Valley. There are other courses to enjoy, such as Sea Island and Torrey Pines—along with prestigious private clubs such as Oakmont, Medinah and The Honors Club. These are worth trying to pull any string you find to gain entry.

So enjoy the Top 100 list, try to play as many as you can, and enjoy the rest while reading and discovering the majesty of these magnificent courses.

—ART STRICKLIN

1. A MASTERFUL PERFORMANCE

*"He chose the lowly things of this world
and the despised things."*

1 CORINTHIANS 1:28

Who doesn't love a good underdog story?

On April 8, 2007, the sports world was transfixed by the triumph of unheralded Zach Johnson. A skinny, soft-spoken Christian golfer from Iowa City, Iowa, Johnson won one of the most prestigious tournaments in golf on that day. The 56th-ranked player in the world at the time, Johnson held off four-time champion Tiger Woods on that Sunday to win the Masters, secure his first major title, and capture only the second win of his career.

FAST FACT:

Zach Johnson's 1-over-par 289 equaled the highest score by a Masters champ.

The win at Augusta National propelled Johnson to a fantastic season, which included another win six weeks later (AT&T Classic), three other top-10 finishes, and more than $3.9 million in earnings.

Judging from countless biblical examples, God loves underdog stories. In fact, in His infinite wisdom, He often interacts with humanity in divine paradox. In 1 Corinthians 1:27–28, for instance, Paul says, "God chose the foolish things of the world to shame the wise" and "the weak things of the world to shame the strong."

Think about Joseph, Moses, Samuel, David, the disciples, the apostle Paul —the list could go on and on. All came from humble beginnings. Early on, none of them looked like future patriarchs, kings, or world-changers. But God delights in turning human wisdom upside down to accomplish His purpose "so that no one may boast before him" (1 Corinthians 1:29).

Think about your own life. What's your underdog story? Trace your humble beginnings and identify your own "major victory." Then give glory to the Master for pursuing a lost sinner and making something out of nothing. Thinking in those terms gives a whole new meaning to the term "Master's championship."

— JOSHUA COOLEY

PLAYING THROUGH

Do a study on the lives of three biblical underdogs.

From the Guidebook: Read 1 Corinthians 1:18–31.

NO. 1: AUGUSTA NATIONAL GOLF CLUB, AUGUSTA, GEORGIA
7,270 yards; opened in 1933
Architects: Alistar MacKenzie/Robert (Bobby) Tyre Jones Jr.
Home of the Masters
www.masters.org

2. TOUGH TIMES

Approach Shot:
Persevering through difficulties

"Perseverance must finish its work so that you may be mature and complete."

JAMES 1:4

Golf can be one of those sports that one day is the easiest game in the world, and everything is going right. Then the next day—well, it feels like the hardest game in the world, and nothing goes your way.

A great example in my life was around the 1998 or 1999 season. It seemed like everything I did on the golf course went right. I was constantly improving, and it seemed like the game of golf was easy.

FAST FACT:

In 2002, Aaron Baddeley played on the Nationwide Tour and finished 10th on the money list to earn his PGA Tour card. He has been on the Tour ever since.

Then from 2000 through 2004 for the majority of the time golf seemed so hard. And so did life. It was as if everything I did in practice and on the course didn't work, and if it did work, it was only for a little bit. Nothing seemed to last. It was during this tough time that God started to develop a godly character in me.

Life can be much the same way. We can feel as if life is easy, everyone is nice to us, our job is going well, things are great, and everything just seems to be going your way. Then the next day it's as if someone flicked a switch, and it's the opposite: Your boss is mean to you, the bills are adding up, and no one is returning your calls.

That can be when God develops our character. In James 1:4, God calls us to persevere. The word *persevere* in this verse can also mean "patience."

In the tough times, if we stay close to Him and keep being obedient and continue to practice patience and perseverance, God will make us mature and complete, lacking nothing.

That sounds exciting to me.

—AARON BADDELEY

PLAYING THROUGH

When tough times come, do you get angry or annoyed because things aren't going the way you planned? Or are you humble and asking the Lord to show you what He is teaching you and to change you?

From the Guidebook: Read Philippians 1:6.

NO. 2: PINE VALLEY GOLF CLUB, CLEMENTON, NEW JERSEY; PINE VALLEY COURSE

6,999 yards; built in 1918

Architect: George Crump

Does not hold major tournaments; no room for spectators

3. MENTORS AND FRIENDS

*"Now you are the body of Christ, and
each one of you is a part of it."*

1 CORINTHIANS 12:27

When I first arrived on the scene in the LPGA, I was fortunate to be able to get to know mature Christian golfers such as Betsy King and Barb Mucha. They were just what I needed, because they helped me understand the golf scene as a Christian—with the right perspective.

Barb was an especially key Christian friend my first few years on Tour. Now I can return the favor to others. I feel compelled to mentor the rookies coming out on the Tour and give them a sense of security and support as their sister in Christ.

FAST FACT:
Wendy and her husband, Nate, live on a 300-acre cattle ranch near Spokane, Washington.

I have invited numerous rookies to our Bible Fellowship for a chance to meet some of the players in a noncompetitive setting. A few years ago I invited Jamie Hullett to join me for Fellowship. Jamie can come across as very shy and quiet. She seemed to enjoy the message and the fellowship, but because of how quiet she was I didn't know she was already a Christian. She is a very strong follower of Christ and just goes about her walk in a quiet manner.

One year I invited Jody Niemann-Dansie to the group. Jody was not a Christian but through some mentoring by Siew Ai Lim, Jody and her husband, Bryan, became Christians that summer. I simply bridged the gap and befriended Jody by going to dinner and playing practice rounds with her. Then Siew Ai, who has much more mentoring knowledge than I do, had one-on-one Bible study times with Jody.

That's how the body is supposed to work—all working toward a common cause: to let others know the great love Christ has to offer us.

—Wendy Ward

PLAYING THROUGH

List three people you might be able to mentor over time. What steps can you take to begin to help them grow spiritually?

From the Guidebook: Read 2 Timothy 2:1–15.

NO. 3: PACIFIC DUNES, BANDON DUNES GOLF RESORT; BANDON, OREGON

6,633 yards; built in 2001
Architect: Tom Doak
Overlooks the Pacific Ocean shoreline
www.bandondunesgolf.com

4. CALLAWAY AND CALEB

"I am still as strong today as the day Moses sent me out."
JOSHUA 14:11

The man who gave us Big Bertha golf clubs and other great golf gear called it a day in May 2001. On that day, Ely Callaway retired after having led the hugely successful Callaway Golf Company since 1982.

You're probably thinking, *Big deal, people retire all the time.* True. But Ely wasn't some young punk 65-year-old. He retired at the age of 81!

In an age when people seem determined to retire early or to make a million by the time they're 40 so they can drift around the Caribbean, Mr. Callaway kept his eyes on the course. Although he had been planning to step down in the last quarter of 2001, some nagging health issues encouraged him to make an "early exit."

FAST FACT: *Callaway named the Big Bertha golf clubs after a World War I cannon.*

However, ever the prepared business professional, Ely already had the right man ready to take his place when he stepped down. His thoughts on retiring? "If we carefully and intelligently take advantage of these opportunities, our future has never looked brighter."

To have that kind of vision as an octogenarian may not be typical, but it's not unique. A man named Caleb possessed it too. Caleb, as you recall, was one of two spies who encouraged the Israelites to proceed into the Promised Land of Old

Testament fame (Numbers 13). Ten other spies who had gone with them trembled in their boots.

As the years wore on, Caleb stayed strong and true both physically and spiritually. He said in Joshua 14, "So here I am today, 85 years old! I am still as strong today as the day Moses sent me out; I'm just as vigorous to go out to battle now as I was then" (vv. 10–11).

Be a Caleb—regardless of your age or circumstance, choose to serve God faithfully for all your years.

—TOM FELTEN

PLAYING THROUGH

Today, call or e-mail a senior believer you know who is a modern-day Caleb. Thank him or her for the example set and ask for advice on staying strong and true in Christ.

From the Guidebook: Read Joshua 14.

NO. 4: CYPRESS POINT GOLF CLUB, PEBBLE BEACH, CALIFORNIA; CYPRESS POINT COURSE

6,536 yards; built in 1928
Architect: Alistar MacKenzie
On the edge of the Pacific Ocean

5. A COSTLY MISTAKE

"Be careful to do what is right in the eyes of everybody."
ROMANS 12:17

The news stunned golf fans around the globe: On the final day of the British Open, Ian Woosnam had received a two-shot penalty for carrying 15 golf clubs to the first tee.

It seemed impossible that a veteran player could make such a silly mistake. This had never happened to the leader of a major tournament before. The limit is 14 clubs, not 15—it's a basic rule of the game. How could Woosnam and his caddie have missed it?

FAST FACT:
Not only can you not have more than 14 clubs, you have to play a round with the 14 clubs you started with—unless you break one legally. Then you can replace it as long as you don't borrow it from another golfer.

Obviously, they weren't deliberately attempting to break the rules. It was just carelessness. They weren't paying attention. Woosnam received a lot of sympathy from the fans. Who hasn't made a careless error at some point or another?

But as Woosnam discovered, carelessness can cost you. It cost him the lead in the tournament—which he never regained. Without the penalty, he might have finished second instead of tying for third—a difference of $350,000. Woosnam also dropped out of the Top 10 in the rankings, jeopardizing his position on the Ryder Cup team.

Such a little mistake. Such a big price tag.

Like Woosnam, some of us have grown careless in life. We've not been paying attention, and we're in danger of making some serious mistakes. Haggai 1:7 tells us, "This is what the Lord Almighty says: 'Give careful thought to your ways.'"

Over and over in Scripture, God warns us to be careful to follow His rules. He doesn't want us to suffer the painful consequences of disobedience. If we're wise, we'll heed the warning and stay alert, avoiding those costly, careless errors.

—CHRISTIN DITCHFIELD

PLAYING THROUGH

Are there areas of your life where you have been careless lately? If something comes to mind, write it down and pray about it. Ask God to help you be more careful in this aspect of your life.

From the Guidebook: Read Romans 13:1–7.

NO. 5: OAKMONT COUNTRY CLUB, OAKMONT, PENNSYLVANIA

7,229 yards; built in 1903
Architect: Henry Clay Fownes
Host of the 2010 Women's US Open; hosted 2007 Men's
    US Open
www.oakmont-countryclub.org

6. THIRD-GRADERS AND SHEPHERD BOYS

Approach Shot:
Overcoming less-than-favorable conditions

"I come against you in the name of the Lord Almighty."

1 Samuel 17:45

Five high school boys swaggered onto the putting green in Campbellsville, Kentucky, talking about the upcoming golf season. One said, "I heard we might be getting a new player this year." "Oh yeah, who's that?" another smugly replied. Just then they turned to see the "new kid." They stood dumbfounded. It was a third-grader named J. B. Holmes!

This was not a trick. J. B. was *that* good. By the time he was in the eighth grade, little J. B. was hitting the ball a whopping 300 yards. He would go on to earn 10 varsity letters on his high school golf team, and he is now a force on the PGA Tour. He tied for tenth in his first PGA tourney in 2006 and also won the FBR Open, pocketing $936,000.

"I was a third-grader playing with the varsity, so I learned to not get intimidated," says Holmes. "You just do your best and play your game and see what happens."

The Philistine army swaggered back and forth taunting their enemy, the Israelites, to come and fight. "Give me a man and let us fight each other!" shouted their nine-foot-tall prize-fighter, Goliath of Gath (1 Samuel 17:10). Just then the Philistines turned to see a young boy named David approach the battle line. He must have looked like a third-grader compared with the Big G. Armed with just a staff and a slingshot, David would not only defeat Goliath with five small stones but he would also go on to become the greatest king of Israel. David said, "You come against me with sword and spear and javelin, but I come against you in the name of the Lord Almighty" (1 Samuel 17:45).

Will you be among the small in stature who have larger-than-life faith? Believe God . . . play your game . . . and see what happens!

—MOLLY RAMSEYER

PLAYING THROUGH

What holds you back from believing God for big things in your life?

From the Guidebook: Read 1 Samuel 17.

NO. 6: PEBBLE BEACH GOLF LINKS, PEBBLE BEACH, CALIFORNIA

6,828 yards; built in 1919

Architects: Jack Neville and Douglas Grant

Host of 2010 US Open; hugs the rugged Pacific Ocean coastline

www.pebblebeach.com

7. NEW SEASON, NEW GOALS

"The Spirit intercedes for the saints in accordance with God's will."

ROMANS 8:27

One of the great things about sports is that you get to start over each season. You and everyone else begin the season exactly the same. No matter how well or poorly you played last season, when that first ball gets teed up in the first tournament of the season, everybody is at zero.

FAST FACT:

Since joining the LPGA Tour in 1996, Ward has earned more than $4 million during her career.

When I begin a new golf season on the LPGA Tour, I have two goals in mind as I look at my schedule and plan my year. I want to set goals that continue to push my talent forward, but I also want to keep in rhythm with the goals and direction God has planned for me.

At the beginning of each calendar year, I sit down and pray about what God wants to accomplish through me. In the back of my mind I have evaluated the previous year's goals, which I placed before God last year. I like to set challenging goals, but in accordance with God's will for my life. If my goals are pleasing to Him, then the Holy Spirit inside of me will allow me to feel good about my direction for each new year. I have to be comfortable with my goals on the inside before I can attain anything on the outside.

Then I can turn my goals over to God, depending on Him to guide me throughout the season—no matter what happens.

Think about the goals you set—whether it's for school, work, or family. Do you make sure to include God in your plans?

—WENDY WARD

PLAYING THROUGH

What were your goals at the start of this year? Is it time for a review? What can you set up for goals that you and God can work on for the rest of the year?

From the Guidebook: Read John 6:38–40. It's about Jesus and His desire to do God's will.

NO. 7: SHINNECOCK HILLS GOLF CLUB, SOUTHAMPTON, NEW YORK

    6,821 yards; built in 1891

    Architect: Willie Dunn; revised by Toomey and Flynn

    Hosted US Opens in three centuries: 1896, 1996, 2004

8. CHASING NO. 1

*"We are the clay, you are the potter; we are
all the work of your hand."*

ISAIAH 64:8

Once a generation or so, a golfer comes along who nearly takes the word *competition* out of the sport.

At one time, that golfer was Byron Nelson. In 1945, the Texas golfer won eleven straight PGA Tour victories. Imagine having to tee it up and face Lord Byron during that streak. You would pretty much be playing for second place.

During the 1960s and 1970s, it was Jack Nicklaus who seemed invincible—winning on the PGA Tour 73 times and capturing 118 tournaments worldwide.

And at the turn of the century it was Tiger Woods who was seemingly unbeatable. Here's how Curtis Strange explained Woods' affect on other golfers when he was at his peak: "These guys have no chance to be No. 1 as long as Tiger's around." And indeed some golfers did feel unmotivated during that time. After all, what's the point if you can't win?

FAST FACT:
*Curtis Strange
was inducted
into the Golf
Hall of Fame
in November
2007.*

Many of us can relate to the frustration of these golfers. No, we don't have to face an unbeatable golfer each week on the links, but there are people at school, at work, at church, or even in our own families who constantly outshine us. No matter what we do, it seems we just can't win. They are faster, stronger, smarter, better. When we compare ourselves to them, we always come up short.

But the Bible tells us that each of us was created by God in His image. He knit us together in our mother's womb (Psalm 139:13). He has given every one of us special gifts and talents. Each of us is unique.

God says He has a plan and a purpose for us (Jeremiah 29:11). In Scripture, He reminds us to focus on Him, not others. Don't be discouraged or intimidated by others' gifts and callings. Focus on doing what God has called you to do.

Don't go chasing the unchaseable.

—CHRISTIN DITCHFIELD

PLAYING THROUGH

List five good characteristics God has gifted you with. Then praise and thank Him for doing that.

From the Guidebook: Read 2 Corinthians 10:12–17 to see how we should direct our comparisons.

NO. 8: WINGED FOOT COUNTRY CLUB, MAMARONECK, NEW YORK; WEST COURSE

7,264 yards; built in 1923
Architect: A. W. Tillinghast
Hosted the 2006 US Open
www.wfgc.org

9. FEEL LIKE A FAILURE?

"God is the strength of my heart."
PSALM 73:26

Do you ever feel like a failure? Former British Open champion Tom Lehman has had that sinking feeling. Here's the pro golfer's story.

When Tom was a fuzzy-faced 15-year-old, his high school football team won the Minnesota state championship. Tom's whole hometown was at the game, and when his team was victorious, 26-7, they went nuts!

FAST FACT:
Tom Lehman has had five PGA Tour victories during his career, including the 1996 British Open.

The team was ushered into the city atop fire trucks, a huge pep rally was held in the school auditorium, and everyone was so happy they were crying.

That is, everyone but Tom.

The fact that he never played a down that season had him down on himself. He felt worthless. He felt like a failure. The football victory only made his inner struggles more painful.

Tom wrestled with questions like, *"Why am I here? What gives life meaning? Why am I so miserable?"*

The turning point came when his coach encouraged him to attend a Fellowship of Christian Athletes meeting. At the youth gathering, he heard other students talking about "unconditional love" and "eternal acceptance."

Tom soon found, in a relationship with Jesus Christ, forgiveness for his sins and a self-image based in knowing a holy, loving, and sovereign God. Before that, Tom thought self-worth was based on accomplishments, but now he knew that it is solely found in God's grace.

Do you struggle with self-doubt or performance-based self-evaluation? Turn to Christ today! You'll find relief from that "failing feeling." He truly will be your hope and strength forever!

—TOM FELTEN

PLAYING THROUGH

Write a letter to God telling Him about your failures and thanking Him for the hope you find in Him!

From the Guidebook: Read Titus 2:11–15.

NO. 9: SEMINOLE GOLF CLUB, JUNO BEACH, FLORIDA
6,787 yards; built in 1919
Architect: Donald J. Ross
Beautiful vistas of the Atlantic Ocean

10. WHAT REALLY MATTERS

Approach Shot:
Finding peace during rough times

"Peace I leave with you; my peace I give you."
JOHN 14:27

The stage was all set for Phil Mickelson. Tied with Payne Stewart on the final hole of the 1999 US Open, Mickelson had to make a birdie putt to claim his first major tournament title. His putt rolled wide. But Stewart faced a fifteen-foot putt, making it seem that at worst Mickelson would get a chance in a playoff. But Stewart calmly sank the putt to claim the championship.

FAST FACT:

Between 1991 and 2014, Mickelson won 42 PGA titles, including the British Open, the PGA Championship, and the Masters (three times).

Mickelson, who had held a one-shot lead only two holes earlier, was devastated. Stewart approached the disappointed runner-up and reminded him that within weeks he would be a father for the first time. Suddenly, a sense of calm came over Mickelson, who smiled at Stewart's consoling comment.

Certainly, there are times when it appears that our lives are falling apart and that everything we have worked so hard for is suddenly out of reach. But then God somehow nudges us and reminds us that since we belong to Him, His peace is at our disposal. In John 14, we learn that peace from Jesus is unlike anything the world tries to offer us. It's a peace that passes all understanding (Philippians 4:7), giving us the assurance that we do not need to let the trials of daily life overwhelm us.

And like Stewart did with Mickelson, sometimes all we need is a timely reminder of what really matters. God's peace is there for the taking. Why not ask for it the next time you find yourself disheartened.

—Jeff Arnold

PLAYING THROUGH

The next time life seems to have you overwhelmed, stop at that moment and pray specifically for God's peace. He has promised to be with us at all times, and He wants us to depend on Him. Pray and ask and see just how God works in the situation.

From the Guidebook: Read John 14.

NO. 10: SOUTHERN HILLS COUNTRY CLUB, TULSA, OKLA-HOMA; FRONT NINE/BACK NINE COURSE

7,085 yards; built in 1936
Architect: Perry Maxwell; renovated, 1999: Keith Foster
Hosted three US Opens and four PGA Championships
www.southernhillscc.org

11. SPEND TIME WITH GOD

"Your face, Lord, I will seek."
PSALM 27:8

"You make it look so easy and graceful."

I have heard this comment about my golf swing many times. Often my response is, "I have played golf for 20 years, hitting thousands of golf balls, stroking thousands of putts, and competing in several hundred tournaments."

I have practiced and spent lots of time developing a graceful swing. It didn't just happen the first time I played golf. I have chosen to spend time honing my golf skills, and in return I have been blessed with the opportunity to play professionally. When I don't spend time practicing, I find it difficult to stay consistent on the course. So I must spend time practicing daily to stay competitive.

FAST FACT:
When she was in college at San Jose State, Hanson's team won an NCAA championship.

I believe the same principle applies to our relationship with God. A strong relationship with Him does not just spring up overnight. One of the reasons God wants us to spend quality time with Him is so we can get to know Him better.

We can do that by studying and reading the Bible, and by learning from mature Christians. Just as I must listen carefully to my golf coach in order to improve my game, we must also spend time talking and listening to God to enhance our relationship with Him. Through intimate moments with God, we grow, we change, we're encouraged, and we find rest. The psalm writer David said, "My heart says of you, 'Seek his face!' Your face, Lord, I will seek" (27:8).

Seek His face daily and allow your spirit to be refreshed and renewed.

—TRACY HANSON

PLAYING THROUGH

Have you spent time with God today? Set aside 30 minutes for the next five days and enjoy God's company. Read Scripture, pray, or just listen to God.

From the Guidebook: Read Psalm 34:1–10 to discover some of the benefits of spending time with God.

NO. 11: MERION GOLF CLUB, ARDMORE, PENNSYLVANIA; EAST COURSE

6,482 yards; built in 1912
Architect: Hugh Wilson
Host of 2009 Walker Cup and 2013 US Open; built to
resemble British golf courses
www.meriongolfclub.com

12. STRONG AND COURAGEOUS

Approach Shot:
Placing complete trust in God

"Be strong and very courageous."
JOSHUA 1:7

I remember it as if it were yesterday. Sunday, September 22, 2002. Final round of the Solheim Cup.

Individual singles matches were all that were left to decide the team winner. I drew Annika Sorenstam, the world's No. 1 female golfer. The media and world thought this was the biggest mismatch of the day. But not for me or my US teammates. Though my support seemed small, it was plentiful. I knew God would never give me anything He and I could not face together.

So with confidence, I entered the match the underdog and played with the strength and fire only the Holy Spirit could ignite. My husband Nate (who was also my caddie), my captain, my team, my family, and friends all offered me the support and encouragement I would need to face this challenge.

I remember going to sleep the night before this final match and being inspired by the great story of David and Goliath (1 Samuel 17). David, like me, was certainly the underdog taking on the big, mighty giant Goliath. Outsized and destined to be defeated, David stood strong, and with the hand of God on his side, successfully defeated Goliath.

Now, David did not have the support of his teammates as I did, but he did prevail thanks to his faith and trust in God. I was fortunate to have the support of my teammates, plus the power of God working through me to match Annika shot for shot. We went on to halve the match, which was like a victory for me—and eventually it helped lead to the win for the US team.

The essence of my story is standing strong in the face of challenges and battles. With God's help, you can be victorious in everything you do—even when things are stacked against you. Be strong and courageous (Joshua 1:7)!

—WENDY WARD

PLAYING THROUGH

What is your biggest opposition today? A meeting with the boss? A job interview? A huge test? An important game? An illness? We all face Goliaths in life. The question is whether we go up against our problems alone or with God next to us.

From the Guidebook: Read 1 Samuel 17.

NO. 12: MEDINAH COUNTRY CLUB, MEDINAH, ILLINOIS; CHAMPIONSHIP COURSE

7,401 yards; built in 1928
Architect: Tom Bendelow
Hosted three US Opens and two PGA Championships; host of 2012 Ryder Cup
www.medinahcc.org

13. EXCLUSIVE CLUBS

"If you show special attention to the man wearing fine clothes . . . have you not discriminated among yourselves?"

JAMES 2:3–4

I like to play golf when it's hot. And when I play golf, I like to be comfortable, so I wear a T-shirt and shorts.

That would not work in many of the exclusive golf courses across the country. That's because a number of elite, exclusive golf clubs require that the folks who tee it up and drown a few golf balls in their water hazards have to wear long pants (no jeans) and a collared shirt. It is important to the folks who run these clubs that everybody looks snazzy as they hack away.

These clubs have every right to do this. They have expectations of their golfers, and the people who pay good money to play those courses feel more comfortable with well-dressed duffers than they do with guys like me who favor comfort over Ralph Lauren.

FAST FACT:
Basic clothing etiquette suggests that what is good for the golf course is not good for the office. Don't wear your golf ware to work.

Sometimes churches are a little like the Bel-Air Country Club (No. 46 on our Top 100 list). These churches, contrary to what James suggests in James 2:1–7, look askance at anyone who attempts to come through their doors without the proper look. Churches have been known to have folks who think anyone with tattoos or the wrong length of hair or scraggly clothes should not be welcomed with the same love as others more scrubbed and polished.

This goes against so much that Jesus taught and the Bible writers recorded. James said this: "Has not God chosen those who are poor in the eyes of the world to be rich in faith?" (v. 5).

Church is like a public golf course, not a private club. Everyone should feel free to walk in the doors without a whiff of discrimination. Let's open our hearts and our churches to those who need a safe place—and a Savior.

—DAVE BRANON

PLAYING THROUGH

Have you ever looked down on someone who came into your church because he or she did not have it all together in the clothing department? Have you ever gone up to someone who appears poorly dressed for church and welcomed him or her warmly?

From the Guidebook: Read James 2:1–7.

NO. 13: BANDON DUNES, BANDON DUNES GOLF RESORT; BANDON, OREGON

6,732 yards; built in 1999
Architect: David McLay Kidd
Spectacular Pacific Ocean views
www.bandondunesgolf.com

14. IN THEIR OWN WAY

Approach Shot:
Spreading God's love

"The latter do so in love, knowing that I am put here for the defense of the gospel."

PHILIPPIANS 1:16

One of the most famous pictures in golf is of 1999 US Open champion Payne Stewart thrusting his fist into the air after winning his first Open title by defeating Phil Mickelson with an 18th hole birdie at Pinehurst Golf Resort.

But look closer at the photo and what you'll see on Stewart's wrist is a black WWJD bracelet, "What Would Jesus Do." It was the popular and flamboyant golfer's way of showing the entire sporting world the change Jesus Christ had made in his life after years of searching.

FAST FACT:

Payne Stewart won two PGA Championships and a US Open title before his untimely death in 1999.

Philippians 1:16 says, "The latter do so in love, knowing that I am put here for the defense of the gospel." In his own way, Stewart was using his most public spotlight to showcase his newfound love and devotion to Jesus Christ and his defense of the gospel.

St. Francis of Assisi once said, "Preach the gospel at all times and when necessary use words." For many athletes like Stewart, who died in a plane crash less than six months after his US Open win, preaching the gospel at all times can mean using creative actions rather than words.

Athletes have written Bible verses on their uniforms or equipment. Golfer Ben Crane puts a verse in the yardage book he looks at as he approaches every hole. Former British Open champion Tom Lehman has put Bible verses in the lockers of fellow Christians to encourage them before their round.

How are you encouraging and spreading God's words to others? You may not have the public spotlight of a Stewart, Crane, or Lehman, but you can affect people you come in contact with every day.

—ART STRICKLIN

PLAYING THROUGH

How can I affect others I come into contact with at home or school every day? How can I, in love, defend the gospel as Philippians 1:6 says?

For Further Study: Read biographies on Payne Stewart (*Payne Stewart*) and former Indianapolis Colts head coach Tony Dungy (*Quiet Strength*), which talk about making your places of work or schooling your personal mission field.

NO. 14: PINEHURST RESORT & COUNTRY CLUB, PINEHURST, NORTH CAROLINA; COURSE 2

7,020 yards; built in 1935
Architect: Donald J. Ross
Hosted Ryder Cup, PGA Championship, US Open
www.pinehurst.com

15. MORE THAN YOU CAN HANDLE

"When I am weak, then I am strong."
2 CORINTHIANS 12:10

At age 21, LPGA pro Terry-Jo Myers was stricken with interstitial cystitis—a rare and painful bladder disease. For 11 years she lived in constant and excruciating pain, keeping her condition a secret from everyone but her family.

When new medications relieved her pain, Terry-Jo planned a big "comeback"—only to suffer two serious back injuries, both requiring surgery. Eventually, Terry-Jo was healthy again. She no longer kept her struggles a secret. Whenever she has the opportunity, she tells her story in hopes of encouraging others who face difficulties of their own. Often, after hearing her speak, someone will exclaim, "I guess God never gives you more than you can handle!"

FAST FACT:
About 700,000 Americans live with the same condition that afflicts Myers— 90 percent of them women.

Terry-Jo understands what they mean. But she has to disagree. "It's *always* more than you can handle!" she says. "You're not ever supposed to get to where you don't need Him."

The truth is, there's no way we can handle the challenges of this life on our own, no matter how hard we try. God wants us to learn to depend on Him daily.

In 2 Corinthians 12:7–8, the apostle Paul talked about his struggle with a problem he called a "thorn" in his flesh: "Three times I pleaded with the Lord to take it away from me.

But he said to me, 'My grace is sufficient for you, for my power is made perfect in weakness.' "

Is there something in your life that you can't handle? A problem you can't solve? Praise God for it! Because when we're weak, He is strong. God's grace really *is* sufficient. Let Him be your strength today.

—Christin Ditchfield

PLAYING THROUGH

What is the biggest challenge you face today? Ask God to help you with this situation. Pray for strength and grace.

From the Guidebook: Read 2 Corinthians 12:7–10 and Philippians 4:12–13.

NO. 15: NATIONAL GOLF LINKS, SOUTHAMPTON, NEW YORK
6,873 yards; built in 1908
Architect: Charles B. MacDonald; Perry Maxwell and Robert Trent Jones redesigned the course
Hosted 1922 Walker Cup

16. THE REAL WINNERS

*"They say, 'Here is . . . a friend of
tax collectors and sinners.'"*

MATTHEW 11:19

After Steve Jones won the 1996 US Open golf tournament at Oakland Hill CC in Bloomfield Hills, Michigan, he accepted the trophy and said to the crowd, "I just thank the Lord Jesus Christ. Even with God on my side, I was still pretty nervous."

In an article for *Sports Illustrated*, John Garrity said this about Jones' statement: "His words drew cheers from the . . . grandstands. But in seminaries, convents, and temples across the land, the response was probably more restrained. The Jesus of the Bible, after all, spent most of His time ministering to losers. The Messiah was conspicuously absent from the luxury boxes and winners' circles of imperial Rome."

FAST FACT:

Steve Jones was quoted in Sports Spectrum *magazine saying that his main goal is "to grow closer to Jesus Christ—to know Him more fully every year."*

I'm sure Steve Jones knows that God does not side only with winners. He was just using the occasion as an opportunity to witness for his Savior.

Jesus associated with all kinds of people, whatever their station in life. He was "a friend of tax collectors and 'sinners' " (Matthew 11:19). I was reminded of this while talking with a wise elderly woman. She said, "I keep thinking of all the common folks Jesus ministered to. We can't forget the common people."

Winners, losers, wealthy, poor—Jesus died for all. Those who choose to trust in Him are the real winners.

— Dave Egner

PLAYING THROUGH

Are you a real winner? No matter what your socio-economic station in life, you need the salvation Jesus offers. Is He your friend?

From the Guidebook: Read Matthew 9:9–15.

NO. 16: OAKLAND HILLS COUNTRY CLUB, BLOOMFIELD HILLS, MICHIGAN; SOUTH COURSE

7,395 yards; built in 1916
Architects: David J. Ross and Rees Jones
Hosted US Opens, PGA Championships, Ryder Cup
www.oaklandhillscc.com

17. GOD'S TROPHIES

"But store up for yourselves treasures in heaven, where moth and rust do not destroy, and where thieves do not break in and steal. For where your treasure is, there your heart will be also."

MATTHEW 6:20–21

When a golfer finally breaks through and wins a PGA or LPGA tournament, he or she is greatly rewarded in a number of ways.

First, there is the huge paycheck that goes to the winner. That is followed by a round of celebrations, a large, public ceremony, and media interviews. But there is something even more special.

Every championship golfer is given a trophy, a memento or a remembrance of that tournament victory. Some tournaments settle for a large, impressive looking trophy. Others opt for something more exotic—a large sword at Bay Hill in Orlando, a red-checkered jacket in Fort Worth and Hilton Head, a blue garment in Hartford or Charlotte, and perhaps most prestigious of all, the green jacket that goes to the Masters winner at Augusta National Golf Club.

FAST FACT:

Tournament winners are often given a solid gold or silver replica of their winning club.

The Bible also speaks of getting a valuable award as well. It's a crown of glory for God's winners. Second Timothy 4:8 says, "Now there is in store for me the crown of righteousness, which the Lord, the righteous Judge, will award to me on that day—and not only to me, but also to all who have longed for his appearing."

While many professional golfers may have a trophy room or memory room of their many wins, the Bible has another storeroom: "But store up for yourselves treasures in heaven, where moth and rust do not destroy, and where thieves do not break in and steal. For where your treasure is, there your heart will be also" (Matthew 6:20–21).

Your most important riches are those you are storing up for heaven. Make sure your best efforts are given to storing them up—for God's glory.

—ART STRICKLIN

PLAYING THROUGH

What are the true trophies in your life and where are they stored? On earth or in heaven?

For Further Study: Read *The Treasure Principle* by Randy Alcorn.

NO. 17: THE OLYMPIC CLUB, DALY CITY, CALIFORNIA

6,842 yards; built in 1927
Architect: Sam Whiting
Host of 2012 US Open (the fifth US Open at
    The Olympic Club)
www.olyclub.com

18. A FULL CONFESSION

*"Every tongue [will] confess that Jesus Christ is Lord,
to the glory of God the Father."*

PHILIPPIANS 2:11

"Hi, my name is Tim, and I'm hittin' it dead right."

We all laughed when our friend offered this goofy impression of how he might start a Golfaholics Anonymous meeting. Golf addicts ourselves, we were discussing what it might take to create godly fellowship among a group like us.

In recent years, the rise in accountability groups has brought confession to the forefront. In line with James 5:16, followers of Christ are confessing their sins to one another and praying for one another, a practice that James noted would bring healing. There's a lot of good in that!

FAST FACT:

One Golfers Anonymous group has this as one of its 12 Steps: "Made a list of all golf courses within an 80-mile radius and became willing to play them all."

But there's another confession that must be included in our three kinds of talk—the talking we do to ourselves, the talking we do to one another, and the talking we do to God in prayer. This is the confessing of Christ as Lord.

When we confess Christ as Lord, we establish our humble place before Him. When we confess Christ as Lord, we recognize His authority over all firmaments and all functions of creation. When we confess Christ as Lord, we replace our sins with His worth. When we confess Christ as Lord, all glory goes to the Father with whom Christ stands.

That is a full confession.

"Yes, His name is Jesus, and He is all that is right."

—Jeff Hopper

PLAYING THROUGH

Is there anything you are keeping from God? Anything you need to confess to Him? Why not start right now?

From the Guidebook: Read Philippians 2.

NO. 18: CRYSTAL DOWNS COUNTRY CLUB, FRANKFORT, MICHIGAN

6,518 yards; built in 1929

Architects: Alister MacKenzie and Perry Maxwell

Crystal Downs captures the beauty of the rolling hills of northern lower Michigan; hosted the 1991 USGA Senior Amateur Championship

19. MAKING GOD'S CUT

*"I write these things to you who believe in
the name of the Son of God so that you
may know that you have eternal life."*

1 JOHN 5:13

At the end of the second round of every PGA Tournament,
there is the 36-hole cut. This cut eliminates half of the
field—the half that hasn't played well enough to make the cut
score for that week. This allows the other half to continue on,
playing for that week's championship.

Making the cut one week does not ensure you will make the
cut another week. There is no carry-over from week to week
on a made cut; you are only judged by what happens each week and in each tournament.

FAST FACT:
*Only Sam Snead
(82) has won
more PGA tour-
naments than
Tiger Woods.*

Golf superstar Tiger Woods holds the all-
time consecutive cuts-made record at 142, having surpassed golf legend Byron Nelson to gain
that impressive record.

On the other end of the spectrum, Masters
champion Ben Crenshaw (1984 and 1995) once
missed 19 straights cuts on the PGA Tour. England's Justin
Rose missed 24 straight cuts in Europe. Each week they fell
just short of the needed cut line to advance to weekend play
and a chance to earn a paycheck.

Thankfully, for the Christian—for those of us who believe
in Jesus Christ and have asked him to save us through His sac-
rificial death—there are no weekly 36-hole cuts for salvation.

First John 5:13 says, "I write these things to you who believe in the name of the Son of God so that you may know that you have eternal life."

To trust Christ means eternal security—not a weekly salvation that can be gained and lost depending on our actions during a certain week. God still expects us to live a righteous and holy life, but being saved means making the cut forever.

—ART STRICKLIN

PLAYING THROUGH

Have you asked Christ to come into your life, making His forever cut? Are you living like you are a child of the King of kings?

From the Guidebook: Read 1 John.

NO. 19: SAND HILLS GOLF CLUB, MULLEN, NEBRASKA
7,089 yards; built in 1994
Architects: Ben Crenshaw and Bill Coore
www.sandhillsgolfshop.com

20. GIFTS FOR GOLFERS

"You know the grace of our Lord Jesus Christ."
2 CORINTHIANS 8:9

All golfers dream of getting at least one hole-in-one during their playing days. But then there's the Mackenzie family from North Wales. They decided to triple their pleasure!

In 2007, within the span of just 24 hours, mother, father, and son all got holes-in-one at the Llanfairfechan Golf Club. Gill, the 45-year-old mother, was the first to get an ace. On the 116-yard ninth hole, her swing led to nothing but cup!

The next day, not to be outdone by his wife, 47-year-old Ray Mackenzie hit a tee shot on the 115-yard 11th hole that resulted in a hole-in-one. To complete the trifecta, son Sam, 14, *also* aced the 11th hole!

Ray remarked, "The tremendous thing is that Sam had bought a pack of balls for Father's Day, and we both got the holes-in-one with balls from the pack." What a gift!

Each believer in Jesus Christ has received a tremendous gift as well. This one, though, far exceeds any other gift on earth. What Jesus provides has eternal consequences. The gift is grace. There was nothing we could do to earn it—no "holes-in-one" we made in order to receive its benefits.

The apostle Paul wrote, "For you know the grace of our Lord Jesus Christ, that though he was rich, yet for your sakes he became poor, so that you through his poverty might become

FAST FACT:
On July 4, 2002, Michael J. Crean of Denver hit a 517-yard hole-in-one at the Green Valley Ranch Golf Club.

rich" (2 Corinthians 8:9). The riches Paul refers to are not material, but spiritual. For we, by God's grace, are now reconciled to God and our sins are forgiven!

Spend some time at the cross today, and thank Jesus again for becoming "poor" so that you might know God's riches. God's grace—what a gift!

—TOM FELTEN

PLAYING THROUGH

Spend five minutes meditating on what Jesus did for you on the cross. End your time by praying to God and expressing your gratitude for His amazing grace!

From the Guidebook: Read 2 Corinthians 8:9–15.

NO. 20: WHISTLING STRAITS, HAVEN, WISCONSIN

7,514 yards; built in 1997

Architects: Pete and Alice Dye

Host of the 2004, 2010, 2015 PGA Championship, the 2007 US Senior Open, and the 2020 Ryder Cup; overlooks the shores of Lake Michigan

21. PLANS FOR PAUL

Approach Shot:
Trusting God's designs for you

"I press on toward the goal to win the prize for which God has called me heavenward in Christ Jesus."

PHILIPPIANS 3:14

Paul Stankowski was sweating. He was pitted against three other young golfers for a match that would determine whether he would continue PGA Qualifying School. His goal was to make the Tour in 1994, and to do that he needed to be one of two guys in the foursome to top the others.

On the first hole, a player got a birdie. The other three, including Paul, did not. This left Paul and the other two players fighting for one remaining spot.

Paul persevered and won the next hole. The Tour was in view! Several years later, Paul Stankowski still wonders what would have happened if he hadn't won that hole. He also ponders why he had success on that fateful day. "I don't know why," he says, "except that it is for now God's place for me. I'm not saying it's His will for me. His will is for me to serve Him wherever I am. Where I am right now is on the PGA Tour."

FAST FACT:
Author John Feinstein penned a book called Tales from Q School: Golf's Fifth Major.

What about the plans God has for your life? Each new day brings opportunities for you to serve God wherever you are in your career and life.

Another Paul, the apostle, wrote, "Forgetting what is behind and straining toward what is ahead, I press on toward the goal to win the prize for which God has called me heavenward in Christ Jesus" (Philippians 3:13–14).

As you persevere this day, commit yourself to serving God with all your heart. Just like with Paul the putter and Paul the apostle, God has plans for you.

—TOM FELTEN

PLAYING THROUGH

Write these words on a Post-it, "Forget the past. Seek God's plans!" and place it in a prominent place where you will see it often during the day.

From the Guidebook: Read Philippians 3:4–14.

NO. 21: COLONIAL COUNTRY CLUB, FORT WORTH, TEXAS; COLONIAL COURSE

7,010 yards; built in 1936

Architects: John Bredemus and Perry Maxwell

Hosted 1991 US Women's Open; host of annual Colonial golf tournament on the PGA schedule

www.colonialfw.com

22. OLDER AND WISER

"We are being renewed day by day."
2 CORINTHIANS 4:16

L ife catches up with us, doesn't it?

Years pass and those glory years of college and young adulthood give way to the middle years. Then one day you wake up and middle-aged people are calling you sir, thirty-somethings are opening doors for you, and the kid behind the counter at McDonald's is asking you if you want the senior discount.

Your 250-yard drives edges down toward 200 yards. Your five-iron fails you far too frequently, and somehow your putter seems a little unsteady in your hands.

FAST FACT:
Arnold Palmer's first win on the pro golf Tour was in 1955— the Canadian Open.

If you aren't there yet, file this away for a few years. You'll need it. But if you are starting to feel the pull of the retirement years and fear that your better days are in the rearview mirror, take a lesson from Arnold Palmer.

In 2011, when he was asked to describe his perfect day, he of course referred to golf. "I can't hit the ball the way I want to," said the then 82-year-old Palmer. But he did not find aging a roadblock to improvement.

"I've decided I'm going to give it a shot this winter at Bay Hill, for my own satisfaction. I'm going to work at it."

And so he did. He kept practicing, seeking to improve. And then at Bay Hill, the octogenarian shot a 79. And he collected his 20th career hole-in-one.

Now, that's the attitude!

Dude's 82, and he still wants to get better.

Let's transfer that over to the Christian life. And let's set aside for a moment the reality that not everyone is a world-class athlete who can still knock down a straight drive off the tee in his or her eighties. There is always opportunity for us as Christians to grow and improve spiritually.

Athletes reach their peak early in life and skills erode, but spiritually we must keep saying, "I'm going to work at it!"

—Dave Branon

PLAYING THROUGH

What are five areas of spirituality about which you hope to improve? How can you make sure you don't "retire" too early?

From the Guidebook: Read 2 Corinthians 4 to see how to understand our "jars of clay" and our challenge to keep moving on for God.

NO. 22: PRAIRIE DUNES, HUTCHINSON, KANSAS
6,598 yards; built in 1937
Architect: Perry Maxwell
Hosted 2002 US Women's Open, 2006 US Senior Open
www.prairiedunes.com

23. A RUINED WALK

"I will ask the Father, and he will give you another Counselor to be with you forever—the Spirit of truth."

JOHN 14:16

"Golf is a good walk spoiled." *—Mark Twain*

"The unexamined life is not worth living." *—Socrates*

"The unexamined swing is not worth making." *—My friend Bill*

Okay, so Bill didn't actually say that. But he might have. And while I tend to agree with the golf-phobic Mr. Twain, Bill enjoys the game for its simplicity and elegance—that, and the chance to get out of the office on sunny days. Or cloudy days. Or days ending with the letter "y."

Recently Bill got a lesson from a golf pro. After just a few minutes, the instructor made some adjustments to Bill's swing. Suddenly a lifelong problem disappeared, and Bill added 20 yards to his drive. The pro told him, correctly, "That's the best swing you've ever made."

Our lives can be a lot more frustrating and humbling than a game of golf. It seems we're always trying to pitch out of a trap or a hazard. Even our best efforts land us in deep water. Life offers plenty of penalty strokes but never any mulligans.

Shouldn't life come with its own "golf pro"?

It does! Those who follow Jesus Christ have an Instructor, the Holy Spirit, who guides us "into all truth" (John 16:13).

FAST FACT:

In golf, a mulligan is a "do-over." No one is quite sure why the name mulligan became associated with repeating a stroke in golf.

We have God's instruction manual, the Bible, to keep us on top of our game. And we have the communication line of prayer, where we can discuss the day's challenges with One who knows the course we're playing.

So often we ask God to take away the hazards. That's not how He works. Rather than removing the rough spots, He works on our swing. Adversity was meant to sharpen our game, not ruin our walk.

—Tim Gustafson

PLAYING THROUGH

Hints for sharpening your game: Read a chapter of Proverbs each day. If you struggle with prayer, pray briefly but often. Establish a good habit by reading God's Word at the same time each day.

From the Guidebook: Read: John 16:12–15.

NO. 23: THE HONORS GOLF COURSE, OOLTEWAH, TENNESSEE
Built in 1983
Architect: Pete Dye
Located north of Chattanooga; hosted amateur tournaments
such as the Curtis Cup and the NCAA Men's Division I
national championship
www.honorscourse.net

24. SMALL FAITH; BIG RESULTS

*"The disciples came to Jesus in private and asked,
'Why couldn't we drive [the demon] out?' He replied,
'Because you have so little faith.'"*

MATTHEW 17:19–20

With his 1999 Ryder Cup team trailing by what appeared to be an insurmountable 4-point deficit, United States captain Ben Crenshaw looked at a roomful of reporters and told them he had a feeling.

The captain was crazy, people thought, knowing just how much of an uphill fight the Americans faced. But Crenshaw, knowing the competitive spirit that lived within the hearts of his team, boldly predicted that something amazing would happen.

And when Justin Leonard sank a 45-foot birdie putt on the 17th hole, the US capped the biggest comeback in Ryder Cup history.

"I never stopped believing," a choked-up Crenshaw said afterwards. "I'm stunned. This is so indescribable."

How amazing to have a faith so deep that anything seems possible and that when the results come, one can't find words to describe it.

In Matthew 17, a man brought his son who had a demon to the disciples while they were with Jesus. After they failed to cast the demon out, the man took the boy to Jesus, who healed the boy. The disciples can't figure out why they couldn't do what the man asked, and Jesus rebuked them because their faith was so small.

Jesus has empowered us with a faith so great that anything is possible. We have to depend on that faith to do God's bidding. And just think—this faith is so much grander and greater than faith in a bunch of golfers!

—JEFF ARNOLD

PLAYING THROUGH

God brings unexpected events into our life not to make us suffer but to see how strong our faith is. The next time it happens, why not stop and pray and ask Jesus to show His power and presence through the circumstance. Fall back on your faith, rely on it completely, and see what the Lord has in store for you.

From the Guidebook: Read Matthew 17.

NO. 24: THE COUNTRY CLUB BROOKLINE, CHESTNUT HILL, MASSACHUSETTS

6,577 yards; built in 1902

Architect: Willie Campbell

Host of the 1999 Ryder Cup and three US Opens (1913, 1963, 1988); located just south of Boston

www.tcclub.org

25. DEFY THE ODDS

"Jesus looked at [the disciples] and said, 'With man this is impossible, but with God all things are possible.'"

MATTHEW 19:26

Bill Preston really ended 2006 with a bang... bang. On December 31, the 61-year-old golfer from New Zealand scored two holes-in-one during the same round of golf!

Preston, who had never had an ace during 50 years of chasing the little white ball, doubled his pleasure on the 4th and 13th holes. He said, "The second one was a shock. I couldn't believe it, nor could the people on the other tee. It was a real thrill." The elated golfer finished the par 72 course with an 80, seven shots under his course handicap of 15.

What are the odds of getting two holes-in-one during one round of golf? Try 9,222,500 to one! Yep, Bill's big swings definitely allowed him to defy the odds.

FAST FACT:
The two holes that Bill Preston aced were both par 3—143 yards and 139 yards long respectively.

I'm glad that God defies the odds—not on the links, but in real life. In Matthew 19, we read the story of a rich young man who struggled with giving up his vast material wealth to follow Jesus. The Lord told His disciples, "It is hard for a rich man to enter the kingdom of heaven" (v. 23).

The men were blown away, for they thought riches were evidence of God's blessing on those He loves. But Jesus showed them that salvation is a work of God that He can perform even when it seems impossible!

Do you know someone who is resistant to God's plan of salvation? Does it seem against all odds that he or she would ever receive salvation? Don't give up praying for this person and reaching out in Jesus' name.

God loves to defy the odds!

—Tom Felten

PLAYING THROUGH

Grab a 3x5 card and write down the names of one or two people you know who are resistant to the gospel. Place the card in your Bible to mark where Matthew 19:26 is located. As you pray for your unbelieving friends on a daily basis, thank God that He can do the impossible!

From the Guidebook: Read Matthew 19:16–30.

NO. 25: BUTLER NATIONAL, OAK BROOK, ILLINOIS
7,335 yards; built in 1974
Architect: George Fazio
Hosted the Western Open from 1974 through 1990

26. AN EYE-OPENER

Approach Shot:
Sharing the love of God

*"Go and learn what this means:
'I desire mercy, not sacrifice.'"*

MATTHEW 9:13

A man left his house for church one Sunday just as his neighbor was loading his golf clubs into his car. "Henry," the neighbor called, "come play golf with me today." Henry answered firmly, "I always go to church on the Lord's Day."

FAST FACT:
*You can find
out about ways
to use golf as
an outreach
ministry by
going to www.
linksplayers.com*

After a pause the golfer said, "You know, Henry, I've often wondered about your church and I really admire your faithfulness. But I've invited you to play golf with me seven or eight times, and you've never once invited me to go to church with you."

What an eye-opener! To all the "Henrys" in today's church, Jesus gives the same challenge He gave to the Pharisees: "I desire mercy, not sacrifice" (Matthew 9:13). In other words, He wants us to show mercy and love to those who need salvation, not just go through the motions of our own religious beliefs. Jesus further explained His mercy by saying, "I have not come to call the righteous, but sinners" (v. 13).

Consider the destiny of people without Christ. Let this stir you to a compassion greater than your comfortable routine or your fear of rejection. Pray for several people or families near you and ask God to love them through you. And, without nagging, invite them to church.

—JOANIE YODER

PLAYING THROUGH

Sometimes the best way to open the door for witnessing is to do something your acquaintance likes to do. List three people you would like to witness to and one special interest for each—something that could be a door opener for you.

From the Guidebook: Read Matthew 9:9–14.

NO. 26: BETHPAGE STATE PARK GOLF COURSE, FARMINGDALE, NEW YORK; BLACK COURSE

7,065 yards; built in 1936
Architect: A. W. Tillinghast
Host of US Open in 2002 and 2009
www.nysparks.state.ny.us

27. A BUCHAREST PERSPECTIVE

Approach Shot:
Knowing what is most important in life

"Has not God chosen those who are poor in the eyes of the world to be rich in faith?"

JAMES 2:5

Hall of Fame golfer Betsy King has given of herself for the past few years traveling to Europe—especially to Romania—to help children and provide spiritual assistance. She tells about one such experience.

Eight other players on the LPGA Tour and I first went to Romania not knowing exactly what we would be doing. We were with a group that had been involved in adoptions of children in the United States.

The first time we went, we stayed with families and visited orphanages. We got to meet quite a few children, and we played with the kids and supplied some support to the ministry that was working there.

FAST FACT: *Betsy King won six LPGA majors during her remarkable career—including the US Open twice.*

The second time we went, we again went to some orphanages and to a hospital. We sang for the children, which wasn't our forte. We sang for youth groups and at a formal church service in Bucharest.

The thing that stood out as we take these trips is the word *perspective*. We have to put things into perspective in terms of what's really important in life.

The first year, I went to Romania after winning a tournament in Japan, and within 48 hours I was on the streets of Bucharest, meeting street kids—kids as young as five years old who had no place to live. God used that to show me that winning a golf tournament isn't all that important.

We sang the song, "Give Thanks," and one of the lines is "let the poor say I am rich," and for them, it is so true. They're so financially poor, yet they're rich in their faith and commitment to the Lord.

Now, that's a great perspective!

—Betsy King

PLAYING THROUGH

Have you ever considered traveling to another country to show others Christ's love? Check out one ministry that combines sports and overseas mission: Score International. Look up Score online at www.scoreinternational.org.

From the Guidebook: Read James 2:1–13.

NO. 27: SAN FRANCISCO GOLF CLUB, SAN FRANCISCO

6,716 yards; built in 1915
Architect: A. W. Tillinghast
Extremely private course with old-school characteristics

28. FIRST THINGS FIRST

Approach Shot:
Making sure God is No. 1

*"Seek first his kingdom and his righteousness,
and all these things will be given to you as well."*
MATTHEW 6:33

I learned the importance of putting God first in my life fairly early in my spiritual journey.

During my senior year at the University of South Carolina, my focus in life started turning to "me." I had finished my junior year as a first-team All-American and SEC Player of the Year in golf, and I was looking forward to my senior year as being just as successful. I had big plans, and I thought I had everything mapped out for a successful year. Unfortunately, as I got more absorbed in all the things I needed to get accomplished, I forgot about the importance of keeping my daily time with the Lord.

FAST FACT:
Siew Ai Lim finished the 2004 season Number 63 on the LPGA money list—up from 146 in 2003—her best finish.

As my senior year wore on, I completely neglected my quiet times with God, and I became discontented with my life. It wasn't that I totally forgot about God or denied being a Christian. I still went to church and hung around Christian friends. What I didn't do was spend the necessary one-on-one time with God to keep my focus on what God wanted me to do.

I was fortunate, however, to have close friends to remind me about keeping God first. After shifting my focus back to God, the things of life became less significant in the bigger frame of things. With my perspectives back in order, I was able to finish my senior year with the right mindset and place sixth in the NCAA Division I national championships.

It is not that God doesn't want us to set high goals or become successful; He does. But first, He wants to be involved with our lives, and He wants us to include Him in our successes—then He can rightfully get the glory.

—SIEW AI LIM

PLAYING THROUGH

What has been sneaking its way to No. 1 in your life, shoving your relationship with God down the list? What can you do today and this week to make sure things get put back in place?

From the Guidebook: Read Numbers 18:8–29.

NO. 28: PASATIEMPO GOLF CLUB, SANTA CRUZ, CALIFORNIA; PASATIEMPO COURSE

6,439 yards; built in 1929

Architect: Alister McKenzie

Scottish designer McKenzie owned a home on the outskirts of this course

www.pasatiempo.com

29. INFINITELY MORE

*"[God] is able to do immeasurably more than
all we ask or imagine."*
EPHESIANS 3:20

God is amazing, and His plan is perfect. We should never doubt His ability to take us further than we could ever imagine.

There have been times in my life when I couldn't say those words with conviction. But now I am amazed as I look back and recall the tough circumstances God has used to teach me that His power working in and through me can do infinitely more than I could have ever asked or believed.

FAST FACT:
While at the University of Oregon, Ben was a three-time All-Pac-10 golfer.

There have been many defining moments in my career that have taken me further than I could have ever dreamed—simply because I learned to allow God's power to make the difference in me and my golf game. I have learned, as Paul did, that "when I am weak, then I am strong" (2 Corinthians 12:10). Not only have I seen God's touch on my golf but in my relationships with others as well.

So why would I want to limit God? If He is omniscient and all-powerful, then I can believe Him to do those things in my life that seem like impossible dreams to me. When we are in the middle of those difficult times, I need to believe His Word and not my negative thoughts. I need to remember that God's Word promises to cause me to rise above my circumstances.

God has a plan for my life—and it is good! He wants to partner with me in reaching for "more than all we ask or imagine." And He wants to partner with you too! Will you let Him?

—BEN CRANE

PLAYING THROUGH

Reflect back to an accomplishment you were able to achieve that seemed impossible at first. What did God do to partner with you in making that dream a reality? Can you think of anyone in the Bible who was able to do something impossible because of God's power in his or her life?

From the Guidebook: Read 2 Chronicles 20 about King Jehoshaphat.

NO. 29: BALTUSROL GOLF COURSE, SPRINGFIELD, NEW JERSEY; LOWER COURSE

7,221 yards; built in 1922

Architect: A. W. Tillinghast

Host of US Open (seven times in 20th century),
US Women's Open (1961, 1985), PGA Championship
(2005, 2016); named for a farmer named Baltus Roll,
who was murdered in 1831 on the land where the
course would eventually be built

www.baltusrol.org

30. NEVER GIVE UP!

*"We know that suffering produces perseverance;
perseverance, character; and character, hope."*

ROMANS 5:3–4

Seven long years. For seven years I played on the Futures Golf Tour, waiting for my chance to play on the world stage of the LPGA. It took seven attempts at qualifying before I gained my card to play on the Tour. Seven times I went to qualifying only to be disappointed at the conclusion of play that I had not gained LPGA status. Each of those years I learned hard lessons about what it really means to persevere.

My prayer to God about golf went something like this. "God, You gave me a dream to play golf. God, please don't put me on the LPGA until I'm ready and can handle the pressures." There were times when I wanted to quit, give up, and let the dream go. But God always reminded me that it was never "if" I would make it, only "when." He would lead me where I needed to go. In the process, I learned perseverance. It was tough, but now I am so thankful.

FAST FACT:
Kristen graduated from the University of Missouri with majors in English and philosophy.

I learned that when God gives you a dream, hold on to it until He says let go. Pursue it with all the passion you can muster until the Lord says stop. Whether your dream is to be a professional athlete, have a family, be in a relationship, become closer to God—whatever it is, never, ever give up. No matter what God has planted in your heart, hold on to it. The road may be hard, but the lessons learned along the way are priceless.

—KRISTEN SAMP

PLAYING THROUGH

What dream has God planted in your heart? What are you doing right now to passionately pursue your God-given dream?

From the Guidebook: Read Romans 5:1–11.

NO. 30 SPYGLASS HILL GOLF COURSE, PEBBLE BEACH, CALIFORNIA

6,862 yards; built in 1966
Architect: Robert Trent Jones Sr.
Located on the Monterey Peninsula; considered among the
toughest courses on the PGA Tour
www.pebblebeach.com

31. WHEN THE CHEERING STOPS

*"Your Father in heaven is not willing that any
of these little ones should be lost."*

MATTHEW 18:14

An October 2, 2007, interview with PGA legend Seve Ballesteros, in the British Newspaper *The Guardian*, describes the angst that consumed him as, at age 50, he agonized over whether or not to retire from the sports career he cherished.

"I felt very alone," Ballesteros said, describing the final stages of his career, which portrayed a lackluster player instead of the former star on the Tour. "I was virtually retired from serious golf," the three-time British Open and two-time Masters champion told *The Guardian*, "But inside I was not accepting it. There was still confusion in me."

FAST FACT:
Seve Ballesteros was diagnosed with a brain tumor in 2008. He died in May 2011 at the age of 54.

Leaving the familiar and journeying into the unknown can lead to feelings of anxiety. As we face decisions about our future, at times we might feel alone and confused to the point where we question God's role in the details of our lives. But we don't need to be concerned. He truly does care.

Matthew 18:12–14 says, "What do you think? If a man owns a hundred sheep, and one of them wanders away, will he not leave the ninety-nine on the hills and go to look for the one that wandered off? And if he finds it, I tell you the truth, he is happier about that one sheep than about the ninety-nine that did not wander off. In the same way your Father in heaven is not willing that any of these little ones should be lost."

Jesus Christ is concerned about Seve Ballesteros. Jesus Christ is concerned about you. He is concerned about me. He is our Shepherd, who not only guides us into relationship with God but also guides us in the direction we take on earth. Looking for the next step? Trust the One who cares.

—ROXANNE ROBBINS

PLAYING THROUGH

Talk to a friend who made a transition about how he or she received guidance from the Lord in the process.

From the Guidebook: Read Proverbs 3:5–6.

NO. 31: ARCADIA BLUFFS GOLF CLUB, ARCADIA, MICHIGAN

7,298 yards; built in 1999
Architects: Rick Smith and Warren Henderson
Overlooks Lake Michigan's shoreline
www.arcadiabluffs.com

32. FAITH PLUS

"The only thing that counts is faith expressing itself through love."

GALATIANS 5:6

Sport psychologist David Cook gives seasoned golfers one key line of training. He tells them they must "see it, feel it, and trust it." His idea is that they must visualize what they desire to do with a shot, and then they must trust their swing to pull it off. He's telling golfers to have faith in what they have trained their bodies to do through hours of practice.

That's an important concept, because it reminds us that faith is not all in our head or even all in our heart. Faith must be expressed by action to make a difference.

FAST FACT:

David Cook has served the NBA's San Antonio Spurs as "mental training coach."

In fact, the apostle Paul was adamant enough in this regard that he told the Galatians that faith expressing itself in love is "the only thing that counts" (Galatians 5:6).

Many believers have been mystified by the whole idea of faith. Why not? For if faith is "the substance of things hoped for, the evidence of things not seen" (Hebrews 11:1, KJV) there is much room for mystery.

But here is one thing we know to be true: If our faith is unseen, it has no value. We must *act* in faith. We must do what God tells us, even building a curious boat in the middle of the desert, laying our child on a mountain altar, or entering a den of lions.

Why must we do this? To follow Christ, who did what God told Him even when that meant going to the cross.

Like Christ, we must act on our faith.

—JEFF HOPPER

PLAYING THROUGH

What acts of faith do you think would be good for you to do in the next few days? How else can you take your faith from an idea to an action?

From the Guidebook: Read Hebrews 11.

NO. 32: MAUNA KEA GOLF COURSE, KAHUL-KONA, HAWAII

6,737 yards; built in 1966

Architect: Robert Trent Jones Sr.

Contains vistas of snow-capped mountains and the roiling Pacific Ocean

33. BETTER THAN A CADDIE

Approach Shot:
Valuing the work of the Holy Spirit

*"But when he, the Spirit of truth, comes,
he will guide you into all truth."*

JOHN 16:13

When I play in golf tournaments, I always have my caddie with me. The role of the caddie is varied. He gives me the yardage to the pin, helps me pick the right club, gets the direction of the wind, and reads putts. He is also an encourager. There are many things he assists me with on the golf course.

We are a team. I know I can trust him and that he always has my best interests in mind. I ask Pete for advice, and I can choose to listen and take what he says into account before hitting the shot—or I can choose to do it my way.

The Holy Spirit is somewhat like that.

The Bible says that when we are born again, we receive the gift of the Holy Spirit, who dwells within us. The Holy Spirit is far better than a caddie, because He knows everything; He knows the truth.

FAST FACT:
At one time, Aaron's dad, Ron, was the chief mechanic for Mario Andretti's race team.

In 1 Corinthians 2:9–10, Paul said, " 'No eye has seen, no ear has heard, no mind has conceived what God has prepared for those who love him,' but God has revealed it to us by his Spirit. The Spirit searches all things, even the deep things of God."

It is the Holy Spirit who will show us the will of God. We need to take the time to ask Him, listen to Him, and then be obedient to Him.

Jesus called the Holy Spirit the Comforter, Counselor, Helper, Intercessor, Advocate, Strengthener, Standby. A caddie is good to have in golf, but the Holy Spirit is the ultimate guide. He always has your best interest at heart and will always be there for you, because He loves you.

—AARON BADDELEY

PLAYING THROUGH

During the day when you are facing a decision or need help at work or on the course, ask the Holy Spirit to help you. He wants to help. You just need to ask.

From the Guidebook: Read Romans 8:1–17.

NO. 33: BARTON CREEK GOLF COURSE, AUSTIN, TEXAS; FOOTHILLS COURSE

7,125 yards; built in 1985

Architect: Tom Fazio

Cliffs-lined fairways, waterfalls, and limestone caves mark this unusual course

34. LET GO OF YOUR EGO

Approach Shot:
Setting up correct priorities

"Clothe yourselves with humility toward one another, because, 'God opposes the proud but gives grace to the humble.'"

1 PETER 5:5

In the sports world in general and sometimes in the golf world, there is a startling lack of humility.

Athletes often exalt themselves over others. There is too much use of the word "I" and not a lot of thanking those who helped these athletes to their position in the sport.

There is, however, one female professional golfer who is determined to challenge athlete egotism with a selfless attitude toward herself and her great accomplishments.

FAST FACT:

Lorena Ochoa was the first female golfer in nearly a decade to supplant Annika Sorenstam as the No. 1 female golfer in the world.

Mexico native Lorena Ochoa did what many thought impossible. She dethroned the once unbeatable Annika Sorenstam as the No. 1 female golfer in the world. She captured the Ladies British Open in 2007 at storied St. Andrews, was named US Female Athlete of the Year for all sports, and won the National Sports Prize in Mexico for the second time.

With dozens of tournament wins and millions of dollars in prize money, she has earned the right to boast in her abilities, but her Christian faith is more important to her than self-proclamations of greatness.

"Before I play every tournament, I vow to do it all for God. I don't know if there is a word to express it in English, but I want to honor Him," she has said. Ochoa is known for her quiet smile, gracious interaction with the crowd, and her willingness to go out of her way to greet the people not often in the spotlight, including the grounds crew.

"God is always very important to me, my family is important, and then there is golf. That is the way it will always be," Ochoa said.

How are those priorities arranged in your life? Is humility your starting point?

—ART STRICKLIN

PLAYING THROUGH

Are you prideful about some God-given ability? Do you have too much pride about some material possessions that can be taken away in a hurry?

From the Guidebook: Read Proverbs 8–16 for God's discussion of pride.

NO. 34: KAPALUA GOLF CLUB, LAHAINA, HAWAII; PLANTATION COURSE

7,411 yards; built in 1991
Architects: Ben Crenshaw and Bill Coore
Host of PGA Mercedes-Benz Championship
www.kapaluamaui.com

35. AMEN CORNER

"Consider it pure joy, my brothers, whenever you face trials of many kinds."

JAMES 1:2

For more than 70 years the world's greatest golfers have had to face "Amen Corner" en route to the coveted green jacket. The phrase was coined in 1958 to describe the notoriously difficult stretch around the 11th, 12th, and 13th holes of the Augusta National Golf Course where the Masters Tournament is played each year. These troubling holes come at a time in the round when things are either won or lost. If you play them well, you've got a chance of breaking par. But play them badly, and you're in trouble. Whether you are Mickelson, Woods, or Palmer, Amen Corner is the real heartbeat of the Masters—the turning point heading into the home stretch.

All of us face amen corners in our lives—critical times when executing the simple things really seem to matter. No one enjoys difficult stretches in life, but it's there that our character is determined. The Bible says to, "Consider it pure joy, my brothers, whenever you face trials of many kinds, because you know that the testing of your faith develops perseverance. Perseverance must finish its work so that you may be mature and complete, not lacking anything" (James 1:2-4).

FAST FACT:
Sports Illustrated writer Herbert Warren Wind borrowed the term "Amen Corner" from a 1936 song called "Shoutin in that Amen Corner."

What does the amen corner in your life look like? Is it a long grueling par four? Is the wind swirling viciously in your face? Trust God and return to the simple things. "Do the things you did at first" as the church at Ephesus was told in Revelation 2:5. The greatest players are determined in the most difficult of stretches.

—Molly Ramseyer

PLAYING THROUGH

What three simple things can you do during a difficult time in your life to make sure you are heading in the right direction?

From the Guidebook: Read the story of Job and consider the "corner" God took him through in his life.

NO. 35: SHADOW CREEK, NORTH LAS VEGAS, NEVADA

Built in 1990

Architect: Tom Fazio

Deserts and mountains surround the gardens and waterfalls that mark this course

www.shadowcreek.com

36. I HATE TO LOSE

*"A patient man has great understanding,
but a quick-tempered man displays folly."*

PROVERBS 14:29

In 1946 Ben Hogan missed a 3-foot putt on the 72nd hole to lose the Masters at Augusta. Herman Keiser wore the green jacket that day in April. It was the second close defeat at the Masters for Hogan, and he didn't like to lose.

But who does? Those of us who play sports don't like to lose. We like to win. But when you do lose the game, match, or race, do you lose something else? Your temper? I don't know if Ben lost his temper after missing that 3-foot putt. I might have lost mine in that situation. Golf will test more than just your swing sometimes. Losing at any sport will test your character.

FAST FACT:

Ben Hogan won 64 tournaments, including nine majors.

According to the guys who wrote the book called Proverbs, we've lost more than the game, match, or race if we lose our temper. In chapter 14 the writer says that a hothead stockpiles stupidity (v. 17). Losing your temper adds to the stupidity pile in your life. The bigger the better isn't the best when it comes to being stupid.

On the other hand, if you put the brakes on your anger, you'll develop a deeper understanding of self-control and godliness. You'll have wisdom that will set you apart from others. And that wisdom will help keep your life on track (Proverbs 14:8).

Losing the game, match, or race is one thing, but don't lose the double-header. Don't lose your temper too.

—Dan Deal

PLAYING THROUGH

If you've been losing the double-header lately, here's a strategy for winning the temper game: 1. Value wisdom. See the good that wisdom accomplishes (Proverbs 14:1, 8, 23); 2. Live a holy, honest life (Proverbs 14:2, 11); 3. Watch your step and avoid evil (Proverbs 14:16).

From the Guidebook: Read Proverbs 14 every day for a week. What you'll lose you didn't need and what you'll gain will be easy for everyone to see. Want more? Read one chapter of Proverbs for each day of the month.

NO. 36: PECAN VALLEY GOLF CLUB, SAN ANTONIO, TEXAS

7,010 yards; built in 1963

Architect: Press Maxwell

Host of the 50th PGA Championship in 1968

www.pecanvalleygc.com

37. IMPROVE YOUR LIE

"Speak truthfully."
EPHESIANS 4:25

L ongtime friends Greg and Dave head out to the course for a quick nine holes. They come to the ninth tee with Greg up by one stroke. Dave's drive finds the center of the fairway, while Greg pushes his tee shot into the right rough. They look and look but cannot find the ball. Desperate, Greg shoots a quick glance at Dave to see if he's looking and then drops a ball from his pocket.

"Oh, here it is!" Greg shouts triumphantly.

Dave looks at his friend with great disappointment.

"After all the years we've been friends," Dave says, "and you'll cheat just so you can beat me."

"What do you mean?" Greg retorts. "My ball is right here! What makes you so sure I'm cheating and lying?"

"Because," Dave replies, "I've been standing on your ball for the last five minutes!"

Two cheaters!

FAST FACT:
Ironically, 82 percent of executives say they "hate" people who cheat at golf.

A recent survey found that 82 percent of American senior executives admit to cheating at golf. The most popular transgressions include secretly moving the ball to a better position and taking shots over without penalty.

Unfortunately, their dishonesty isn't confined to the golf course. Eighty-six percent of golfing executives admit they also cheat in business. They've given a whole new meaning to "improving your lie."

In a world where lying and cheating is the norm, Ephesians 4:25 calls Christians to be different. "Each of you must put off falsehood and speak truthfully." Followers of Christ need to have a conviction about telling the truth—all the time.

—Brian Hettinga

PLAYING THROUGH

The next time you're tempted to lie to make yourself look better, think about which is more important to you—a good reputation as an honest person or scoring one stroke better.

From the Guidebook: Read Ephesians 4:17–25.

NO. 37: WADE HAMPTON GOLF CLUB, CASHIERS, NORTH CAROLINA

> 7,154 yards; built in 1987
> Architect: Tom Fazio
> Named after a former governor of North Carolina; WHGC is
> a private course with no more than 300 members
> www.wadehamptongc.com

38. FAILURE: AN EVENT, NOT A PERSON

Approach Shot:
Letting God work through loss

"And we know that in all things God works for the good of those who love him."

ROMANS 8:28

According to Mulligan's Rules of Golf: "No matter how badly you are playing, it is always possible to play worse."

But after the final hole of the 1991 Ryder Cup, I think it would have been hard to convince Bernhard Langer that it could get worse. The Ryder Cup is the Super Bowl of golf, and Langer was in the anchor position for the European team. He and Hale Irwin of the US were the last players on the course.

FAST FACT:

In his second year on the Champions Tour (age 50 and over) in 2008, Langer finished second on the money list.

Irwin had bogeyed the 18th, and Langer was faced with a 6-foot putt for par to win the match and retain the Cup for Europe. The Ryder Cup had come down to the last putt on the last hole in the last match on the last day. But in that moment of a lifetime, Bernhard Langer tasted failure. The ball slid over the right edge of the hole and stayed out. Langer said, "All I could feel was pain, agony, and disappointment."

Fortunately, Bernhard Langer understands that failure is an event, not a person. Because of his personal relationship with Christ, he was able to look at the experience from an eternal perspective and cope with it. Later he commented, "I looked at it this way. There was only one perfect Man in this world, and they crucified Him. All I did was miss a putt."

Are you having a hard time getting past a failure? You know, God has a history with people who have failed. Do you love God? Then remember this: In all things, God works.

—BRIAN HETTINGA

PLAYING THROUGH

Hebrews 11 is God's "Hall of Faith," but every person listed experienced a major failure in life. It takes enormous faith to believe that our failures are for the greater good. And by the way, Bernhard Langer, 1991 Ryder Cup "failure," was elected to the World Golf Hall of Fame.

From the Guidebook: Read Romans 8.

NO. 38: KIAWAH ISLAND RESORT, KIAWAH, SOUTH CAROLINA; OCEAN COURSE

7,937 yards; built in 1991
Architect: Pete Dye
Located on a barrier island off the coast of South Carolina;
    host of 2007 Senior PGA and 2012 PGA Championships
www.kiawahresort.com

39. REAL POWER

"Blessed are the meek."
MATTHEW 5:5

The name Jack Nicklaus carries some serious power in the golf world. As a 73-time PGA winner and as a world-class golf-course designer, he's pretty much done it all.

Nicklaus, quoted in a magazine article, noted that the world of golf has changed over the past four decades. He notes that the 18th hole of Muirfield Village, a course he designed in the 1970s, was made for a proper drive of 250 yards from the tee. But at a PGA event held at that same golf course in May 2003, Jack watched as Tour players drove the ball some 315 yards on the 18th hole—into the wind. They totally bypassed the bunkers and other obstacles he had built into the course.

FAST FACT:
Jack Nicklaus' first PGA win was the 1962 US Open, which he captured at the age of 22.

Today, he says, the golf game is much more about power than it used to be. Finesse is still needed—ya gotta have that great short-game to win. But power gets you onto the green.

Our society is consumed with power. The games we play, the DVDs we rent, the things we buy—they're all affected by our drive for more of it.

Jesus, however, in His presentation of the beatitudes, gave us a different view of power. He said, "Blessed are the meek, for they will inherit the earth"

(Matthew 5:5). Meek, in this verse, suggests gentleness and self-control. In other words, power under control.

Instead of listening to the world's messages about power, take Jesus' view to heart. Treat people with gentleness and keep your strength in check. That's real power.

—Tom Felten

PLAYING THROUGH

As you watch TV tonight or listen to the radio or read the newspaper, keep track of how often power is presented. Talk with your family or a friend about your findings and also about Jesus' view of real power.

From the Guidebook: Read Matthew 5:1–12.

NO. 39: MUIRFIELD VILLAGE GOLF CLUB, DUBLIN, OHIO

7,221 yards; built in 1974
Architect: Jack Nicklaus
Host of the Memorial Tournament
www.thememorialtournament.com

40. GUESS WHO IS WATCHING?

Approach Shot:
Realizing you can't hide from God

*"Does he not see my ways and
count my every step?"*

JOB 31:4

Our integrity is tested by what we do when nobody's looking. If we resist stealing, for example, when no one would ever find out, we are honest.

Golfer Raymond Floyd was getting ready to tap in a routine 9-inch putt for par when he accidentally touched the ball with his putter. According to the rules, if the ball moves, the golfer must take a penalty stroke. Yet consider the situation. Floyd was among the leaders in a tournament with a top prize far exceeding $100,000. If he fessed up, the penalty stroke could cost him a lot of money.

FAST FACT:
Raymond Floyd won 22 PGA tournaments from 1963 through 1992.

Writer David Holohan describes what he could do: "The athlete ducks his head and flails wildly with his hands, as being attacked by a killer bee; . . . all the while [looking for] any sign that the ball's movement has been detected by others. If the coast is clear, he taps the ball in."

Ray Floyd didn't do that. He assessed himself a penalty stroke and wound up with a bogey.

Read about Job in chapter 31. He knew how useless it was to try to hide things from God. He maintained his integrity by fearing God and turning his back on evil thoughts. He could have cursed God for all the terrible things that happened.

Remember, he lost his livestock, his children, and his health. But he kept his heart pure. Pleasing God was really what mattered the most to Job.

Are we as sensitive to doing what's right? Are we as intent on being true to God, even when others aren't looking?

Whatever we do, God is in the audience! Pleasing Him is what really matters.

—MART DeHAAN

PLAYING THROUGH

Is there anything you're hiding from God? Get it out in the open today (God knows about it anyway), and ask Him for forgiveness and help.

From the Guidebook: Read Job 31:1–8.

NO. 40: RIVIERA COUNTRY CLUB, PACIFIC PALISADES, CALIFORNIA

6,950 yards; built in 1927

Architects: George Thomas and William Bell

Host of the US Open, the PGA Championship, and the Nissan Open among its many tournaments over the years; several movies have been filmed at the Riviera

www.rccla.com

41. BETTER PUTTING & MORE

Approach Shot:
Improving your relationship with God

"Put on the new self, created to be like God in true righteousness and holiness."

EPHESIANS 4:24

It should come as no surprise that there's an App for improving your putting.

Most of us have long since given up keeping track of the number of Apps that can be purchased for our phones. But for golfers, what can be better than iPing, which advertises itself as being able to "Lower Your Putting Handicap."

Now, before you put down this book to go order this App for yourself, let's talk about what it does. Applied to your smart phone and attached to your putter, it "measures," which means it monitors a series of putts you take and then shows you where your stroke needs improvement. And then it shows you what you need to "practice."

That's an App we all need as golfers, isn't it? We'd all be excited to have what amounts to a personal putting coach.

But would we be as excited about having an "App" that measures our spiritual life and then tells us how to practice it properly? There is one, and you don't need a smart phone to use it. The measurement part of this application is found in Psalm 139:23-24, where David says, "Search me, O God, and know my heart; test me and know my anxious thoughts.

See if there is any offensive way in me, and lead me into the way everlasting." How is that for being measured? Ask God to reveal to you where you are going wrong. And remember, this is written by a man who did some major wrong things—and then when God revealed them to him he repented and got back on the right track.

And what about the practice part of this App? A good place to go for help here is Ephesians 4 and 5. As you read from 4:22 through 5:21, you'll see lots of "practice" pointers—ways to put into practice the life God wants you to live.

Measurement and practice. It's a great App for both putting improvement and spiritual growth.

—DAVE BRANON

PLAYING THROUGH

Take a notebook and begin "measuring" how you are doing spiritually. Then begin "practicing" new ways of growing in faith.

From the Guidebook: Read Ephesians 4:22–5:21.

NO. 41: PRINCEVILLE GOLF CLUB, PRINCEVILLE, HAWAII (KAUAI ISLAND)

7,309 yards; built in 1990
Architect: Robert Trent Jones Jr.
Overlooking the Pacific Ocean and Hanalei Bay on Kauai's north shore
www.princeville.com

42. ZACH'S MARKER

Approach Shot:
> Pointing toward God

"God also testified to it by signs, wonders and various miracles, and gifts of the Holy Spirit distributed according to his will."

HEBREWS 2:4

Before the 2007 Masters, Christian golfer Zach Johnson retreated to Sea Island, Georgia, the home of his golf instructors, for a complete skill tune-up before the season's first major championship.

For several days, Johnson worked on his putting and chipping, driving and iron play. He did everything with his coaching team to get ready to win the year's most prestigious major.

FAST FACT:

Zach Johnson set a course record at the East Lake Country Club in 2007 with a third-round score of 60 during The Tour Championship.

Before he left the training session, Johnson was given a ball marker by his sports psychologist Morris Pickens. A ball marker is a coin golfers use to mark their ball on the green if they have to pick up their ball.

One side of the small marker had the Bible verse Matthew 6:33–34: "But seek first his kingdom and his righteousness, and all these things will be given to you as well. Therefore do not worry about tomorrow, for tomorrow will worry about itself. Each day has enough trouble of its own."

The other side had Proverbs 3:5–6: "Trust in the Lord with all your heart and lean not on your own understanding; in all your ways acknowledge him, and he will make your paths straight."

Pickens told Johnson that every time he put down his ball marker during the Masters, he wanted him to see those verses as a sign God loved and cared for him regardless of his golfing situation.

When events of life combine to make things stressful for you, what are the signs you look at? What are you depending on for help?

Zach Johnson won the Masters that year, and afterwards he pointed to God to give Him the glory. What are you pointing to?

—ART STRICKLIN

PLAYING THROUGH

Do you have a life verse that you can quote to sum up your life? Do you have a sign to point to when things get tough?

From the Guidebook: Search the Bible to find a verse that best sums up your faith and life. Adapt it as your own and depend on it to remind you of God's work in your life.

NO. 42: EAST LAKE GOLF CLUB, ATLANTA, GEORGIA
7,267 yards; built in 1915; renovated in 1995
Architects: Donald Ross and Rees Jones
East Lake is the permanent home of The Tour Championship

43. "THE NEXT SHOT IS THE BIG ONE!"

Approach Shot:
Moving beyond your mistakes

"Forgetting what is behind and straining toward what is ahead."

PHILIPPIANS 3:13

In the Scripture reading for today (see "From the Guide-book"), the apostle Paul gave us the secret to moving forward in the Christian life. We are to set our eyes on the goal and keep looking ahead. When we look back to our past sins or shortcomings, we open the door to discouragement.

I find a rather embarrassing parallel in my golf game. A twice-a-week golfer at most, I don't play enough to perfect my swing or to master all the shots. In every round, therefore, I make mistakes. A drive will go astray. An iron shot will splash beautifully into the creek. Or a putt will break left when I was sure it would break right. Because of that, I appreciated these words by Grantland Rice in his book *The Tumult and the Shouting:* "Because golf expresses the flaws of the human swing—a basically simple maneuver—it causes more self-torture than any game short of Russian roulette. The quicker the average golfer can forget the shot he has dubbed or knocked off line—and concentrate on the next shot—the sooner he begins to improve and enjoy golf. Little good comes from brooding about the mistakes we've made." Rice then commented, "The next shot, in golf or in life, is the big one."

FAST FACT:
Grantland Rice also said, "Golf gives you an insight into human nature, your own as well as your opponent's."

Has some sin in your past got you down? Do you find yourself often brooding about it? Are you discouraged about some failure? Confess it to God, claim His forgiveness, and put it behind you for good. In the Christian life, as in golf, the next shot is the big one!

—DAVE EGNER

PLAYING THROUGH

What flaw in your Christian life is bothering you right now? What do you think you should do about that particular item?

From the Guidebook: Read Philippians 3:12–16.

NO. 43: TROON NORTH GOLF CLUB, SCOTTSDALE, ARIZONA; PINNACLE COURSE

7,044 yards; built in 1991
Architect: Tom Weiskopf
Considered one of the top desert courses

44. A TIMELY WORD

*"A man finds joy in giving an apt reply—
and how good is a timely word!"*

PROVERBS 15:23

In Liverpool, England, on the eve of the 2006 British Open championship, professional golfer Graeme McDowell was in trouble. The next day he was going into the tournament clueless about what was causing his struggles on the course.

FAST FACT:

Graeme McDowell finished 11th in the 2005 British Open. In 2006, he finished 61st after leading with a first-round 66.

While he was out for the evening, McDowell got a surprise. A stranger, who was an avid golf fan, recognized him and commented that he had noticed a flaw in Graeme's swing. The next day, Graeme tested that advice on the driving range, and to his great shock he discovered that the fan had been correct. Satisfied with the value of the change, Graeme implemented the suggestion and finished the first day of the British Open in first place! All because a stranger took time to speak a word of help.

Words are like that. They are powerful instruments for good or for ill. We can use words in destructive ways, or we can use words to build and encourage. This must be what Solomon had in mind when he said, "A man finds joy in giving an apt reply— and how good is a timely word!" (Proverbs 15:23).

In a world where words are often wielded as weapons, may we use our words as tools to build up the hearts of others.

— BILL CROWDER

PLAYING THROUGH

Who needs a word of encouragement from you today? Can you e-mail, text, call, Facebook, or deliver face-to-face that message of hope before you forget?

From the Guidebook: Read Ephesians 4:17–32.

NO. 44: WE-KO-PA GOLF CLUB, FORT MCDOWELL, ARIZONA; SAGUARO COURSE

> 7,225 yards; built in 2006
> Architects: Ben Crenshaw and Bill Coore
> We-Ko-Pa is owned by the Fort McDowell Yavapai Nation of Native Americans
> www.wekopa.com

45. CASEY'S EXAMPLE

*"This happened so that the work of God
might be displayed in his life."*

JOHN 9:3

All Casey Martin wanted to do when he was growing up was play golf for a living. He loved the game, showed some natural ability, and was encouraged by his dad and his family to chase his dream. It was the same encouragement he was given in his local church outside of Portland, Oregon.

But early in his golfing career, he discovered he had a rare blood disorder in his leg. He could not walk long distances; his blood pooled in his leg and made extended physical activity, especially golfing, difficult and painful.

FAST FACT: *Casey Martin became the golf coach at the University of Oregon in 2006.*

As Martin continued to pursue his professional golfing dream, the pain in his right leg continued to get worse. He was often fearful of losing his leg or seeing his golfing dream end.

Martin said a college girlfriend helped him see how God can use any obstacles in life to glorify Himself.

"She pointed out the story of the man born blind in the Bible and how we can honor God regardless of the situation," Martin explained. "She made the point that I should use my leg and whatever God gave me to honor Him."

After long struggles with his leg and golfing ability, along with a protracted legal battle to gain the right to play pro golf, Martin achieved his goal of playing on the PGA Tour.

While he never achieved the fame or victories he might have with two "perfect" legs, Martin was able to overcome the obstacles in his life by relying on his faith in God and honoring Him with everything he did.

What are the obstacles in your life? What are you using to overcome them? Allow your faith in Jesus Christ to help you, as did Martin and many others, to achieve your best for Him.

—ART STRICKLIN

PLAYING THROUGH

What obstacles can a faith in Jesus Christ help you overcome? Are there any barriers that you have to live with? How can God be honored?

From the Guidebook: Read Job in the Old Testament. See the purpose of trials and God's glory in life.

NO. 45: CHICAGO GOLF CLUB, WHEATON, ILLINOIS

6,574 yards; built in 1892

Architect: Charles B. McDonald

Oldest 18-hole golf course in North America; has hosted the US Open and the Walker Cup

46. DAILY DEVOTION

Approach Shot:
Staying connected to God

"Sing to the Lord, praise his name;
proclaim his salvation day after day."

PSALM 96:2

Tiger Woods has won many dramatic tournament victories during his professional golf career. But one of his greatest achievements went virtually unnoticed because it unfolded slowly over seven years. During that period, Tiger made it through qualifying in 142 consecutive tournaments. No player in PGA history had ever gone to as many US professional golf tournaments without missing the cut. That streak speaks to the power of his commitment to golf, the consistency he developed through long years of practice, and his conviction not to give up improving his game. Whatever else we may know about Woods, this one thng is true: When it comes to golf, he is devoted.

Recently I was challenged by a friend's statement of his growing desire to follow the Lord with "daily rather than dramatic devotion." Is that how it is in my life of faith in Jesus Christ? Am I consistent or erratic? Am I dependable or unreliable?

There are great spiritual events in our lives, but our daily choices to obey Christ best express our ongoing love for Him. Psalm 96, a ringing call to witness and praise, says, "Sing to the Lord, praise his name; proclaim his salvation day after day. Declare his glory among the nations, his marvelous deeds among all peoples" (vv. 2–3).

When we are consistently devoted to the Lord, we will proclaim His love and power day after day. Over time, a life of daily loyalty will become a magnificent testimony to our Savior.

— David McCasland

PLAYING THROUGH

In what area of your spiritual life do you feel inadequate? What daily spiritual discipline do you think could help you with that? Make a plan to incorporate that into your life.

From the Guidebook: Read Psalm 96.

NO. 46: BEL-AIR COUNTRY CLUB, LOS ANGELES

6,482 yards; built in 1926

Architect: William P. Bell

Not for everyday people, Bel-Air is a course for the rich and the famous—and people who don't wear jeans or shorts while playing golf (it's in the dress code); among those who have played the exclusive course: Dr. Phil, Joe Namath, Pete Sampras, and Vin Scully

www.bel-aircc.org

47. THE VALUE OF ONE

Approach Shot:
Investing in others

*"The things you have heard me say in the presence
of many witnesses entrust to reliable men who
will also be qualified to teach others."*

2 TIMOTHY 2:2

When Harvey Penick died at the age of 90 in 1995, the world of golf lost one of its greatest teachers. Although his books have sold millions of copies, he was remembered most for his direct impact on people.

An Associated Press story stated, "Penick refused to teach methods or group lessons, instead applying his wisdom to the talents of individual players." Tom Kite, who won $11 million on the PGA Tour, was 13 when he began working with Penick. Ben Crenshaw, who had 19 PGA wins, began learning the game from Penick at the age of six.

FAST FACT:
Penick's Little Red Book *is the highest selling golf book ever published.*

Penick, who could have spent his life speaking to crowds, chose to invest himself in people—many of them children—one at a time.

The apostle Paul modeled this kind of unselfish mentoring relationship with a young man named Timothy. Then he urged Timothy to do the same with others. He wrote, "The things you have heard me say . . . entrust to reliable men who will also be qualified to teach others" (2 Timothy 2:2).

Face to face—person to person—one to one. This is the most effective way of teaching. It goes beyond the telling of facts to communicating genuine interest and love.

Why not begin today to invest yourself in someone who needs a spiritual teacher, mentor, and friend?

— David McCasland

PLAYING THROUGH

Who are three people in whose lives you would like to invest? What can be a good first step in making a difference in their lives?

From the Guidebook: Read 2 Timothy 2:1–7.

NO. 47: AUSTIN COUNTRY CLUB, AUSTIN, TEXAS

6,906 yards; built in 1912
Architect: Pete Dye
Austin Country Club was Harvey Penick's home course

48. SOMETIMES 100TH, SOMETIMES FIRST

Approach Shot:
Seeking God's "well done"

"You have been faithful with a few things."

MATTHEW 25:21

Betsy King is one of the most decorated women in golf history. She has received just about every accolade her sport has to offer. Her career began some three decades ago and has earned her prestigious Hall of Fame status, 34 LPGA victories, and more than $7.6 million in career earnings. Betsy King knows how to give 100 percent, and she knows what it means to be No. 1.

But beyond her remarkable career, King remains grounded in her strong belief in Jesus Christ. She says, "God wants us to give 100 percent, but that's it! We don't have to get all caught up in being No. 1. If we're highly talented and become No 1, fine. But if we give our best, and we're No. 100, that's fine too. Sometimes we finish 100th. Sometimes first."

FAST FACT:
Betsy King has helped to raise more than $1.1 million to give to various charities!

Matthew 25:14–30 tells us the story of three men who were entrusted with various amounts of money before the man who gave it went away on a trip. To the man who had given his 100 percent effort, his master tells him, "Well done, good and faithful servant! You have been faithful with a few things; I will put you in charge of many things" (Matthew 25:21). What talent has God entrusted to you? Are you giving it your 100 percent effort, or are you wasting your treasure? No matter how athletic or how smart or how gifted you are, use the resources that God has given you and hear your Master say, "Well done." Sometimes you finish 100th. Sometimes first!

—MOLLY RAMSEYER

PLAYING THROUGH

Are you more concerned about being the best or trying your best? And for whose glory are you making this effort?

From the Guidebook: Read Matthew 25:14–30. Which servant do you most resemble?

NO. 48: THE BOULDERS GOLF CLUB, CAREFREE, ARIZONA
6,811 yards (North), 6,726 yards (South); built in 1994
Architect: Jay Morrish
Interesting rule at The Boulders: If a coyote steals your ball,
you can replay the shot

49. SERIOUS STROKES

Approach Shot:
Learning to serve others

"Each one should use whatever gift he has received to serve others."

1 PETER 4:10

David Sullivan was exhausted after a recent session of hitting the little white ball. I can't blame him, for he used drives and putts to play *a 1,100-mile hole!* The 42-year-old roofer took three months to golf his way across the United Kingdom—from John o' Groats (northern Scotland) to Lands End (southern England).

FAST FACT:
Sullivan thought his golf "fundraiser" would require just 24,000 shots. Boy, was he wrong!

"I've been up mountains, in gardens, chased by bulls—you name it. My feet are killing me," Sullivan said after completing his unusual feat. Why would someone whack away at golf balls (he lost 293 along the way) for three months? To raise big bucks for two local children's charities.

Nice job, David. We hope you get some positive strokes after having amassed 247,387 of your own during your golf odyssey.

The true tale of David Sullivan is a good reminder of what it means to "give it up" for others. As believers in Jesus, we are called to live out selfless lives that benefit the people around us.

In 1 Peter 4, the apostle wrote, "Above all, love each other deeply" (v. 8). When we show true love to fellow Christians, they are blessed, and unbelievers see the reality of Jesus in us.

Peter developed this idea when he wrote, "Each one should use whatever gift he has received to serve others" (v. 10). The

Holy Spirit has given every believer a specific gifting that will benefit the whole body of Christ.

What "strokes" have you been using to serve others? How have you been using your Spirit-given gifting to build others up?

It's time to use what God has given you!

—Tom Felten

PLAYING THROUGH

Ask someone close to you what he or she feels is your spiritual gift. Pray and ask God to use your gift to serve others through the power of the Holy Spirit.

From the Guidebook: Read 1 Peter 4:7–11.

TOP 100

NO. 49: FLINT HILLS NATIONAL GOLF CLUB, ANDOVER, KANSAS

6,900 yards; built in 1997
Architect: Tom Fazio
Fazio calls Flint Hills "as good a course as I've ever designed."
www.flinthillsnational.com

50. IN THE ROUGH

*"The reason I left you in Crete was that you might
straighten out what was left unfinished."*

TITUS 1:5

The game of golf teaches us, among other things, that we can't always take the easy way out of a difficult situation. When a tee shot rolls off the fairway and into the rough, for instance, the golfer has a problem. He can't just pick it up and place it where it will be easier to play. No matter how difficult the lie, the ball must be hit from the rough.

FAST FACT:

The Pro Golf Shop Web site gives this suggestion for hitting out of a rough: To give more control over the shot and lessen the effect of the grass on the backspin, stand more ahead of the ball than usual and take a steeper swing so that less of the grass is involved.

Young Titus found himself "in the rough." He had been left in Crete, charged with the task of building up the Lord's work there. But he was encountering problems. The Cretans were generally deceitful, immoral, and lazy, and this spirit had invaded the churches where problem people were causing division. It is possible that a discouraged Titus had written to Paul, asking for a transfer to some easier field of service.

Whatever the situation, Paul realized that his friend needed encouragement, so he began his letter by saying, in essence, "Yes, things are bad in Crete. But that's exactly why I left you there. God can use you to bring about great and necessary changes." In golf terms, he had to play Crete where it was lying. Titus listened to Paul, and he succeeded. Although the Bible record doesn't give us the results of this encouraging letter from Paul, archeologists have found the remains of stately churches that had the name "Titus" inscribed on their cornerstones.

Christian, when you are in a difficult place, you won't be helping yourself by looking for the easy way out. Instead, trust God and face up to the challenge! Battle your way through the problem. You'll become a better person, and you'll discover that God can make you a winner!

—HERB VANDER LUGT

PLAYING THROUGH

Are you facing an "in the rough" situation? Did you ever think that perhaps God has you there for a reason?

From the Guidebook: Read Titus 1.

NO. 50: SHOAL CREEK COUNTRY CLUB, BIRMINGHAM, ALABAMA

Built in 1977
Architect: Jack Nicklaus
Host of two PGA Championships and the US Amateur

51. SECOND-CHANCE CHAMPIONS

Approach Shot:
Learning from your failures

*"By faith Abraham . . . offered Isaac as a sacrifice.
He who had received the promises was about
to sacrifice his one and only son."*

HEBREWS 11:17

The Senior PGA Tour is also called the Champions Tour. Some refer to it as the "Second-Chance Tour." It has given many long-time teaching pros a new golfing career after age 50.

FAST FACT:

The all-time leading money winner on the Champions Tour is Hale Irwin.

Sportswriter Jack Cavanaugh says, "In no other sport does an athlete who never made it to the world-class level in his prime get a second chance in middle age to prove himself and amass riches that he could only dream about in his 20s, 30s, or 40s."

Are you looking for a second chance? There's a widespread idea that if you once miss "God's best" you can never again render gold-medal service to Him. But in Hebrews 11, faith's "Hall of Fame," we read of several who failed yet came back strong for the Lord.

Abraham, often willful and impatient in waiting for the son God had promised, demonstrated amazing faith in offering up Isaac (vv. 17–19). Jacob, the schemer who stole his brother's birthright and blessing, became a man of faith who blessed his children and worshiped God (v. 21). Moses spent 40 years in Midian before leading God's people out of Egypt (vv. 24–28).

Our previous mistakes do not necessarily exclude us from serving God. His best for us is that we turn away from our sin, learn from our failures, and begin anew to follow Christ. That's the way to be a second-chance champion.

— David McCasland

PLAYING THROUGH

In what area of life do you feel that you need a second chance? Do you think God is willing to give that to you? What steps do you need to take to grow closer to Him and accept His help?

From the Guidebook: Read Hebrews 11:17–32.

NO. 51: ESTANCIA CLUB, SCOTTSDALE, ARIZONA

7,146 yards; built in 1995

Architect: Tom Fazio

Built around an exclusive gated community in the Arizona desert

www.estanciaclub.com

52. GRIP, STANCE, FOLLOW-THROUGH

*"For you were once darkness, but now you
are light in the Lord."*

EPHESIANS 5:8

Several years ago, I attended a mini-clinic taught by professional golfer Wally Armstrong. I was pleased to learn that he is a Christian and that he has a solid grasp on the meaning and purpose of the Christian life. He expressed his convictions in a talk to the people at the clinic, using golf to tell of his beliefs.

Armstrong talked first about grip, how the golfer holds the club. If the starting point, the grip, is bad, the golfer's entire game will suffer. He drew a parallel with our grip on life, indicating that the first step is to be born again through faith in Jesus Christ (John 3:16).

FAST FACT:
*You might
want to read
Wally Arm-
strong's book
The Mulligan.*

Next, he spoke of the stance. The way a golfer addresses the ball determines the success of his shots. If his stance is crooked, he will get into trouble. Armstrong likened that to the Christian's daily life. If he takes the right stance, denying sin and committing himself to obey Christ, he will know God's pleasure.

Third, Armstrong advised the serious golfer to have a strong follow-through. If it is short or weak, his shots will not be long or accurate. Likewise, a Christian is to follow through on his commitment to the Lord. He is not to become discouraged but to continue fighting the good fight of faith (2 Timothy 4:7).

Every experienced golfer knows the value of the correct grip, the right stance, and the proper follow-through. But we all need to remind ourselves of how important these elements are in the Christian life.

—DAVE EGNER

PLAYING THROUGH

How's your grip? Are you saved? How's your stance? Are you living for Jesus? How's your follow-through? Are you remaining committed to God?

From the Guidebook: Read 1 Thessalonians 1.

NO. 52: CASTLE PINES GOLF COURSE, CASTLE ROCK, COLORADO

7,559 yards; built in 1981
Architect: Jack Nicklaus
www.castlepinesgolfclub.com

53. TOO SOON TO QUIT

Approach Shot:
Sticking with Christ for the duration

"Let us throw off everything that hinders and the sin that so easily entangles, and let us run with perseverance the race marked out for us."

HEBREWS 12:1

Chris Couch of Fort Lauderdale, Florida, was just 16 years old when he first qualified to play golf at its highest level on the PGA Tour. He was quickly declared the next golfing prodigy and a surefire success for years to come.

Life, however, turned out to be more of a grind. Chris did not enjoy a sprint to success but endured a marathon that would take 16 years and three different stints on "mini-tours." Tempted to quit, Couch persevered and finally, at age 32, became a Tour winner for the first time when he captured the 2006 Zurich Classic at New Orleans in a thrilling finish. His persistence had paid off, but it had not been easy.

FAST FACT:
In 2005, Couch made $96,667 on the PGA Tour; in 2006, his paychecks totaled $1,356,731. Quite an improvement!

In his book *A Long Obedience in the Same Direction*, Bible teacher Eugene Peterson reminds us that the Christian life has much more in common with a marathon than with a 100-meter dash. Peterson says we are called to persevere in "the long run, something that makes life worth living."

With the grace and strength of Christ, we too can "run with perseverance" this race of life (Hebrews 12:1). And with our Lord's example to help and encourage us, we can, like the apostle Paul, run to win the prize of "a crown that will last forever" (1 Corinthians 9:25).

Are you in the middle of a tough battle—one that is taking longer than you anticipated? Keep going. It's always too soon to quit.

— BILL CROWDER

PLAYING THROUGH

Is there some aspect of life about which you feel like giving up because things are tough? What will it take spiritually for you to see the importance of persevering?

From the Guidebook: Read 1 Corinthians 9:24–27.

NO. 53: GRAYHAWK GOLF CLUB, SCOTTSDALE, ARIZONA; RAPTOR COURSE

7,135 yards; built in 1995
Architect: Tom Fazio
Host of PGA Tour event Frys.com Open
www.grayhawkgolf.com

54. WHEN WE CANNOT SEE

*"Trust in the Lord with all your heart and
lean not on your own understanding."*

PROVERBS 3:5

I remember a time when I played in a golf tournament where I did not get the opportunity to see the course before the round. Fortunately, my caddy was familiar with the course. I felt a little nervous and anxious as we began the day since I was not even sure where to find the next tee box! Finally, I decided to trust my caddy. He knew exactly where to hit the ball, how far to hit it, and where all the holes were.

FAST FACT:
Kristen's low round on the LPGA Tour is 68, which she has enjoyed twice—once in 2004 and once in 2005.

On several holes, my caddy would hand me a club, show me the target, and tell me to hit it there. I listened and obeyed. After a few holes, instead of being anxious, I found myself quite relaxed. My caddy had done the hard work of mapping out a plan. I simply had to hit the ball where he instructed.

This is the same trusting attitude we need to take with God. God will always be the best guide for our lives. He wants to direct, teach, and love us. Our challenge is to listen to Him and obey.

God knows best. He knows which paths will take us on the road to blessing and which will cause us added trouble. We cannot see all the hazards that lie before us. That is why we need our all-knowing God.

Trusting in God's perfect plan is the most gratifying way to navigate this life and its challenges. So listen and trust. God knows exactly where you need to hit it!

—KRISTEN SAMP

PLAYING THROUGH

What are some fears that keep you from trusting God? How can you give these fears to God and let Him replace fear with power?

From the Guidebook: Read Psalm 56.

NO. 54: THE PRESIDIO GOLF COURSE, SAN FRANCISCO

6,500 yards; built in 1895; redesigned in 1995

Architect: Arnold Palmer

A public course that is managed with the least possible pesticide use

www.presidiogolf.com

55. WHO'S IN CHARGE HERE?

Approach Shot:
Letting God take control

"Commit your way to the Lord; trust in him."

PSALM 37:5

Trust is a difficult concept to grasp. It is even harder when the chips are down.

I remember the second time I made it through Qualifying School. I had shot 83 the first day, and the prospects of keeping my card on Tour weren't looking very bright. After much prayer and reflection, I decided that there wasn't much I could control, and I decided that I would give the rest of the week over to God.

The only thing I could control was to discipline myself to stay committed and play every shot to the best of my ability. How the rest of the field did was something that I could not control. I knew that God held my future in His hands and that no matter what happened, He knew what was best for me. After deciding that I would yield control to God, a tremendous burden was lifted from me because I knew that I no longer had to worry. All I had to do was my very best and trust that God knew the best plan and way for me.

FAST FACT:
Siew Ai's name is pronounced "See-you I."

The next day I shot a 67, and I picked up my first career hole-in-one. I also played well the remaining two days, and I was able to keep my card for the following season.

There is something freeing about letting go and letting God handle your concerns. It is hard to do, because we all want to exercise some form of control in our lives. If we could just learn to let God be in charge, we would have less to worry about in our lives. After all, He's our Maker. Of course He knows the best plan for our lives.

—Siew Ai Lim

PLAYING THROUGH

What area of your life are you having trouble giving up to God? Is it a matter of trust or a matter of simply not wanting to let go?

From the Guidebook: Read Proverbs 16:1–9.

NO. 55: VIRGINIA COUNTRY CLUB, LONG BEACH, CALIFORNIA
6,505 yards; built in 1919
Architects: William P. Bell and A. W. Tillinghast

56. THE BIBLE: OUR GUIDE TO LIFE

Approach Shot:
Trusting God's Word

"Do not let this Book of the Law depart from your mouth."

JOSHUA 1:8

When I play in a tournament I never played before, I depend on the course book guide. This book maps out every hole in detail—everything from the distance off the tee to a bunker or to water, then on the fairway how far to the green.

The reason for the details is that as professional golfers we know how far we hit the ball with each club. When we know the correct distance to the hole, it helps us to hit the ball close. Also, the book helps us avoid trouble such as sand traps and water.

FAST FACT:
Aaron Baddeley won the 1999 Australian Open as an 18-year-old amateur.

The course book or course guide has a similar role to the one the Bible has in my life. God gave us His Word to help guide us through life, and that is how I use it.

The Bible tells us all the things we need to do to live life the way God wants us too. For instance, the Bible says to have a close relationship with the Lord, to trust Him, to be obedient, to love people, to forgive people, and to be patient.

During each tournament, officials give me a course book to help me with my decisions, but it's my choice to use the book. Similarly, the Lord has given me the Bible for guidance, but it's my choice to read it and put it into practice daily.

That's why in Joshua 1:8 God told Israel's leader to meditate on God's Word day and night.

The Bible is the key to living life the right way. Use it.

—AARON BADDELEY

PLAYING THROUGH

Are you reading your Bible daily? Are you putting into practice what the Bible says? What part of your life do you need to change because of what the Bible says?

From the Guidebook: Read 2 Timothy 3:16.

NO. 56: OAK HILL COUNTRY CLUB, ROCHESTER, NEW YORK; EAST COURSE

6,902 yards; built in 1926

Architect: Donald J. Ross

Host of three US Opens, the 1995 Ryder Cup, the 2003 PGA Championship, and the 2008 Senior PGA Championship

www.oakhillcc.com

57. WHAT TO GIVE GOD

"But remember the Lord your God."
DEUTERONOMY 8:18

I love getting gifts. I get excited about fancy jewelry, nice clothes, and high tech electronics. But there is one gift I long for, hope for, and desire most. It is other people's time. Nothing means more to me than an hour with a friend over a cup of coffee or a long conversation with my family back home.

I believe God is the same way. I believe that more than anything God would simply like some of our time.

Time is the most valuable currency we have. Once you give your time away, it is gone forever. We cannot go to the store and pick up an extra box of time. Where we spend our time marks our character. How we spend our time defines our priorities. And the best investment of our time is to spend it with God.

FAST FACT:
Kristen was the first University of Missouri golfer to qualify for the NCAA tournament as an individual.

Investing our time with God can remind us of some vital things He has done for us. When we spend time with God, we will never forget the battles He fought for us, the strength He gives us, the blessings He has rained on us.

Deuteronomy 8 cautions us to never forget the Lord. If we are not investing our time with God, we will forget. We will falsely believe it was our own power and wealth that got us to where we are. It will become too easy to follow other gods and worship idols.

The next time you want to let God know you love Him, try giving Him one of the best gifts you can give Him: your time.

—Kristen Samp

PLAYING THROUGH

Take an inventory of your time and see where you are investing it. How could you use your time better? In what ways can you give God more of this precious gift?

From the Guidebook: Read Deuteronomy 8.

NO. 57: DALLAS NATIONAL GOLF CLUB, DALLAS, TEXAS

7,326 yards; built in 2002
Architect: Tom Fazio
Located between Dallas and Fort Worth
www.dallasnationalgolfclub.com

58. A SLOW FOURTH

Approach Shot:
Making sure God is No. 1 to you

"You shall have no other gods before me."
EXODUS 20:3

When golf professional Paul Azinger learned in 1993 that he had cancer, he said, "I was in shock. I had thought that Dr. Frank Jobe would tell me they had discovered some form of weird infection in my shoulder or possibly even a stress fracture. The one word I never expected to hear him say was *cancer*."

The good news was that it was curable. Azinger spent some time away from the professional golf tour for chemotherapy and radiation treatments. When the man who's called "Zinger" came back, he was cancer-free and has remained that way ever since.

FAST FACT:
Paul Azinger captained the winning US team in the 2008 Ryder Cup.

When people asked Azinger if golf was still important to him in light of his illness, he said, "Yes and no. Yes, of course golf is important to me. I love the game; it is how I make a living. But no, golf is no longer at the top of my priority list. In fact, it runs a slow fourth. My priorities now are God, my family, my friends, and golf. Golf is no longer my god. Golf is hitting a little white ball. God is my God, and God is a whole lot bigger than golf."

A serious disease has a way of putting things in perspective. First place belongs to the Lord; we are to worship nothing in our lives above Him (Deuteronomy 6:13–19).

Make God No. 1 in your life, and your dearest pastime on earth will become only a "slow fourth."

— Dave Egner

FOLLOW THROUGH

Think of some areas in your life in which you feel God is not No. 1. What can you begin to do about that? Start by writing down two areas and beginning to restructure them to put God first.

From the Guidebook: Read Deuteronomy 6:13–19.

NO. 58: QUAKER RIDGE GOLF CLUB, SCARSDALE, NEW YORK

6,835 yards; built in 1926

Architect: A. W. Tillinghast

According to legend, George Washington—while bivouacking with his Continental soldiers—once slept under an oak tree that stands not far from the 10th hole at Quaker Ridge

www.quakerridgegc.org

59. USE YOUR IMAGINATION!

"Love is patient, love is kind. It does not envy."
1 Corinthians 13:4

There's a golf legend about a soldier who was able to maintain his sanity during years of imprisonment in Vietnam by playing a mental round of golf every day. During each day of his captivity, he would go to a course in his mind and shot by shot, play an 18-hole round. Upon his eventual release, the serviceman was finally able to get back on the course again. To his surprise, his mental "practice" paid tremendous dividends. He bettered his previous average by 20 strokes. Using his imagination made him a better golfer.

It's also possible to become a more loving follower of Christ by using your imagination. Author and seminary president Neal Plantinga calls this looking at people with "the eye of imaginative love." For example, you get behind a pokey driver in the left lane. Your instinct is to punish the person for being pokey. But if you've got imaginative love, you can give him the benefit of the doubt. You can picture her as a grandparent—one of the good ones with cookies and smiles. As a result, you don't gesture. You don't think about running "gramps" off the road, or rolling down your window and hollering at "granny." You give the person room. Loving Christians can be patient and kind when they look at people with the "eye of imaginative love."

FAST FACT:
English seed merchant and entrepreneur Samuel Ryder founded the Ryder Cup in 1927.

Watching the Ryder Cup or the British Open or whatever tournaments may be on TV this weekend may stimulate your imagination and improve your golf game. But here's something better: Reading 1 Corinthians 13 and practicing "imaginative love" may make you a better follower of Christ.

—BRIAN HETTINGA

PLAYING THROUGH

Memorize the 15 characteristics of love in 1 Corinthians 13:4–7.

From the Guidebook: Read 1 Corinthians 13.

NO. 59: MID-PINES INN AND GOLF CLUB, SOUTHERN PINES, NORTH CAROLINA; MID-PINES COURSE

6,515 yards; built in 1921
Architect: Donald J. Ross
www.pineneedles-midpines.com

60. HAVE YOU BEEN SEALED?

*"You were marked in him with a seal,
the promised Holy Spirit."*

EPHESIANS 1:13

Back before I retired from the LPGA in 2009, most Tuesdays would find me driving to the golf course of that week's tournament for a practice round. As I drove through the front gate, I would hold up my money clip. The security person would wave and allow me to enter.

The LPGA Tour money clip is a powerful piece of metal. It had my name inscribed on it along with the words: "Ladies Professional Golf Tour." It signified that I was a member of the Tour, and it enabled me access to anywhere I wanted to go around the tournament site. When I wore the money clip, I received both respect and a right of passage. It was my seal of approval stating that I was a professional golfer.

FAST FACT:
In 2003, Tracy was presented with the Daytona Beach (FL) Kiwanis Foundation Humanitarian of the Year Award.

Unlike the money clip that I had to earn, I have another seal of approval that I experience in my life. This one I got because of nothing I did. When I accepted and trusted Jesus Christ as my personal Savior, God marked me with the seal of His Holy Spirit. This seal gives me full and direct access to God, His promises, and His power.

God tells us in Ephesians 1:14 that the Holy Spirit "is a deposit guaranteeing our inheritance until the redemption of those who are God's possession—to the praise of His glory." For those of us who have trusted Jesus Christ, the seal of the Holy Spirit signifies that we are one of God's children.

Do you have that "seal?" Is the Holy Spirit your guarantee?

—Tracy Hanson

PLAYING THROUGH

Please make sure you are sealed with God's Holy Spirit. If you've never asked Jesus Christ into your heart to forgive you and to save you, do so now. God will mark you "with a seal, the promised Holy Spirit" (Ephesians 1:13).

From the Guidebook: The book of Ephesians has several passages about the Holy Spirit: 1:12–14; 2:18, 22; 4:3–4; 6:17–18. Read those passages and perhaps do a short study of what they teach.

NO. 60: THE CHALLENGE AT MANELE, LANAI CITY, HAWAII

7,039 yards; built in 1993

Architect: Jack Nicklaus

Built on lava fields above high cliffs that plunge to the Pacific Ocean, Manele offers breathtaking beauty on every hole; on Hole No. 12, golfers have to clear 200 feet of ocean to reach the green

www.golfonlanai.com

61. LOVE THAT "SWEET SPOT"!

*"If your brother sins, rebuke him,
and if he repents, forgive him."*

LUKE 17:3

I f you play golf, you know how important it is to hit the ball at just the right spot on the clubface.

That's why the new generation of huge clubs is so helpful to us duffers. Those clubs are more forgiving. The metal-head woods, the featherweight clubs, and the hollowback irons have expanded what is often referred to as the "sweet spot" on the club. Now it is possible to hit the ball on the heel or the toe of the club and still get good distance.

FAST FACT:
The "sweet spot" is largest in a driver, with the size of that spot being about the size of a quarter.

The idea of a golf club that has a large and forgiving "sweet spot" reminds me of how Christians should respond to one another. Instead of being like the old, unforgiving club that required near-perfect performance, we should be like the new clubs that are generous with the faults of the golfer. We should have a large "sweet spot" that provides plenty of room to forgive any repentant brother or sister in Christ (Luke 17:4).

That's the pattern the Lord Jesus set for us.

In fact, He came to earth to die for our sins and to show us, by what He said and did, what forgiveness really means. During His life, and even while He was on the cross, He forgave everyone who called to Him in faith.

We should follow His example. Sure, we can't forgive sins as He does, but we can forgive those who have wronged us. After all, who should be more forgiving than those of us who have needed and experienced so much forgiveness ourselves?

As believers in Jesus, we should have the largest "sweet spot" of all.

—MART DeHaan

PLAYING THROUGH

Do you have a hard time forgiving? What kinds of things are really hard for you to forgive? What are two situations going on right now in which you need to practice forgiveness?

From the Guidebook: Read Luke 17:1–10.

NO. 61: FISHERS ISLAND CLUB, FISHERS ISLAND, NEW YORK; FISHER ISLAND COURSE

6,544 yards; built in 1926

Architect: Seth Raynor

Located at the eastern end of Long Island Sound, this island
is a summer getaway for the wealthy

www.fishersislandclub.com

62. A MATTER OF TRUST

"I trust in you, O Lord; I say, 'You are my God.'"
PSALM 31:14

During his heyday as a golfer, Tiger Woods had a bigger impact on his sport than perhaps any other athlete in American sports history. His success on the course set him apart as perhaps the best golfer ever. If you are old enough, you might recall seeing the very first time Woods was on national television. He was just two years old, and he appeared with his dad on *The Mike Douglas Show*—where he amazed viewers with his golf skills at such an incredibly young age.

FAST FACT:
Andrew Provence played in 69 games during his 5-year NFL career.

Tiger and his father Earl were extremely close. They bonded not only as father and son but also through thousands of hours as player and coach. During the early stages of Woods' career, observers were continually amazed—not just by Tiger's golf performance, but also by the love shared between him and his dad. It was clear that if there was one man in the world Tiger trusted, it was his dad. It's easy to wonder if things might have turned out better for Tiger if his dad had been around longer.

Trust is important in both golf and relationships. Coaches will tell their students that to become a good golfer, a person must learn to trust his swing. And in life, David shared in Psalm 37:5: "Commit your way to the Lord; trust in him and he will do this." Just as Tiger trusted his dad, who taught him his swing, we must trust God to teach us how to live.

He will work in and through us as we commit our way to Him. Because of His unfailing love, our heavenly Father can be fully trusted.

—ANDREW PROVENCE

PLAYING THROUGH

When did you fully commit your life to the Lord? List three things of your life that you desire the Lord to accomplish.

From the Guidebook: Read Psalm 37.

NO. 62: BANDON DUNES GOLF RESORT, BANDON, OREGON; BANDON TRAILS COURSE

6,775 yards; built in 2005

Architects: Ben Crenshaw and Bill Coore

Golf Digest said of Bandon Trails: "Golf in heaven can't compare."

www.bandondunesgolf.com

63. "GOOD SHOT!"

Approach Shot:
Extolling the Lord with praise

"Praise the Lord. I will extol the Lord with all my heart."
PSALM 111:1

The annual golf outing for the men of our church provided a good time of fun and laughter. Slices, hooks, and complete misses provided groans and embarrassment. But whenever someone made a long drive, even the men who usually said very little responded to their partner's success by saying, "Good shot!"

One man kept telling his partner, "Great! Great shot!" Words of praise flowed freely during the whole time, some in loud exclamations, others quietly spoken. But every man knew what it was like to encourage another and to receive praise for an accurate drive or a long putt.

FAST FACT:
While it is good to be complimentary, make sure to obey the basic rules of etiquette and keep the noise down for other golfers on the course.

The psalmist gave many reasons to praise the Creator and Provider of all the blessings of life. He mentioned God's great works (Psalm 111:2), His righteousness (v. 3), His grace and compassion (v. 4), His provision of food (v. 5), His power (v. 6), His justice (v. 7), His faithfulness (v. 8), and His redemption (v. 9). Praise is a compliment to God, and we honor Him when we lavish praise on Him.

If we can compliment a good golf shot or some other small accomplishment, shouldn't we compliment God for His great goodness?

Think of something for which you can say, "Praise the Lord!" Then praise Him all day long.

—DAVE BURNHAM

PLAYING THROUGH

When was the last time you counted your blessings? What are five things you can praise God for right now?

From the Guidebook: Read Psalm 111.

NO. 63: VAQUERO GOLF CLUB, WESTLAKE, TEXAS; VAQUERO COURSE

7,064 yards; built in 2001
Architect: Tom Fazio
Just 385 owner-members play this exclusive course—so exclusive the caddies wear uniforms

64. A FIRM FOUNDATION?

"Everyone who hears these words of mine and puts them into practice is like a wise man."

MATTHEW 7:24

I play golf. I'm always trying to improve my swing—especially my stance. It's the most important element of a golf swing. If I stand with my feet too close together, I'll lose balance; too far apart, and I won't be able to turn the hips properly. A proper stance is foundational to a promising golf swing.

Following Jesus' teachings is foundational to a promising life. Jesus taught that a person who applies His teachings to life will be like a house built on a solid rock foundation. When the environment around the house becomes threatening, the house will withstand because of its strong base. Jesus went on to teach that a person who doesn't apply His teachings will be like a house built on a shaky foundation. When the storms of life blow, that house is in danger.

FAST FACT: George McGovern is the chaplain for both the New York Yankees and the NFL New York Giants.

You and I are in the process of building our lives. It only makes sense to build our lives on a firm foundation. No life is so charmed that it remains free of adversity. That's why our "houses" need to be built on the lessons and views of the Author of Life. He alone knows how to handle the variety of "storms" that invade our space.

Our "houses" are being battered daily. Take a moment, walk down into the basement, and check the foundation. Do you see solid rock? If not, don't worry; it's not too late. Jesus' words are found in the Bible. The Sermon on the Mount would be a good place to start (Matthew 5–7).

—GEORGE MCGOVERN

PLAYING THROUGH

Have you checked your foundation lately? Spend some time evaluating it today—then take any necessary action.

From the Guidebook: Read Matthew 7:24–29.

NO. 64: FOREST HIGHLANDS, FLAGSTAFF, ARIZONA; CANYON COURSE

7,007 yards; built in 1988
Architects: Jay Morrish and Tom Weiskopf
Carved out of the Ponderosa pines in the mountains of
    northern Arizona
www.fhgc.com

65. DON'T BE STUPID

*"Give thanks to the Lord, for he is good; . . . who can pro-
claim the mighty acts of the Lord or fully declare his praise?"*

PSALM 106:1–2

Christian athletes, including golfers, have a long history
of using a post-victory interview with the media to give
grateful praise to God. But when Webb Simpson won his first
PGA title in August 2011 at the Wyndham Championship in
Greensboro, North Carolina, he gave his proclamation an added twist.

FAST FACT:
*Later in 2011,
Simpson also
won the
Deutsche Bank
Open in
Norton,
Massachusetts.*

What Simpson said that day can be a wakeup
call for each of us who claims to have a relationship with God through Jesus Christ. We all can
fall into the "take everything for granted" mode
and forget to thank God for His goodness to us.

Here's what the 26-year-old Simpson said that
day, "I'd be stupid not to thank my Lord and Savior Jesus Christ."

Wouldn't we all be stupid to make that same mistake? Yet
don't we spend far too much time forgetting who provides for
us everything we have?

Let's look at who else says it's unwise not to thank the Lord.

The psalmist: "Give thanks to the Lord, for He is good"
(Psalm 107:1).

The apostle Paul: "Thanks be to God for His indescribable
gift" (2 Corinthians 9:15).

Paul, again: "Give thanks in all circumstances" (1 Thessalonians 5:1).

Whoever wrote Hebrews: "Let us be thankful, and so worship God" (12:28).

If you're having trouble figuring out why it would not be smart not to thank God, perhaps it would be good to review some other, less mundane reasons for giving thanks:

- Salvation through Jesus, promising eternal glories
- A beautiful world in which to live
- Family and friends who love you and care about you
- God's Word, which clearly spells out how to live

The list could go on for a long, long time. But the point is clear: We have so much for which to be thankful. So, let's be smart—let's live with an attitude of thankfulness to God.

—DAVE BRANON

PLAYING THROUGH

When do you feel most thankful? When do you have trouble giving thanks? Should thankfulness depend on circumstances?

From the Guidebook: Read Psalm 107:1–8.

NO. 65: OLYMPIA FIELDS COUNTRY CLUB, OLYMPIA FIELDS, ILLINOIS

7,157 yards; built in 1922
Architect: Willie Park Jr.
Host of the 2003 US Open
www.ofcc.info

66. SOMETHING TO AIM FOR

"Therefore I do not run like a man running aimlessly."
1 CORINTHIANS 9:26

The most important part of hitting a golf shot is having a target to aim at. If I do not have a target, then I do not have direction. Hence, I will not end up in the correct position I need to be in to shoot a good score.

When I pick a target to aim at, I have purpose when I hit the ball because I have a specific place I want it to finish.

In life we too need a target—we need a purpose that we are focused on.

In 1 Corinthians 9:26, Paul said that he didn't run aimlessly. The New Living Translation says, "I run with purpose in every step." When Paul woke up every day, he had purpose in what he was doing. He was focused on doing all that God had called him to do. Philippians 3:14 says, "I press on toward the goal to win the prize for which God has called me heavenward in Christ Jesus."

FAST FACT:
Aaron Baddeley won the 2006 Verizon Heritage Classic on Easter Sunday.

Each time I play golf, I must keep my focus on my target, so I maintain my purpose. I equally must maintain my focus on my calling and continue to be obedient to the calling that God has placed upon my life. I will keep playing golf and telling people about Jesus until He tells me otherwise.

This is what Paul says at the end of his life. "I have fought the good fight, I have finished the race" (2 Timothy 4:7).

Paul lived his whole life with purpose. Are you living with purpose?

—AARON BADDELEY

PLAYING THROUGH

Are you living life with purpose? Are you where God has called you to be? Are you being obedient to what God asked you to do?

From the Guidebook: Read 1 Corinthians 9:24–27.

NO. 66: BLACK CREEK GOLF CLUB, CHATTANOOGA, TENNESSEE

Built in 2000

Architect: Brian Silva

Hosted Nationwide Tour Chattanooga Classic; located northwest of Lookout Mountain in the Lookout Valley

www.blackcreekclub.com

67. COURAGE COUCHED AMONG CRUELTY

*"You see the trouble we are in: Jerusalem lies
in ruins, and its gates have been burned with fire.
Come, let us rebuild the wall of Jerusalem."*

NEHEMIAH 2:17

Over the past few years, the attention of the world turned to the city of New Orleans in her time of disaster and pain. However, the real story has come in her rebuilding and healing process. Inside a cruel world full of unexplainable events, New Orleans is slowly reconstructing herself and showing uncommon courage.

Nestled among that same storm-battered city of New Orleans, Chris Couch's story mirrors that courage. A PGA golf tournament designed to help the city's rebuilding allowed Chris Couch to reconstruct his career.

FAST FACT:

Chris Couch's best year after 2006 was 2011, when he earned more than $900,000 on the PGA Tour.

Couch was ranked 368th in the Official World Ranking at the time, and this tournament would represent his 66th Tour start and his 66th possible failure. Chris was financially broke, down-on-his-luck, and wondering if his chance would ever come. Then something strange happened. Couch played with unbelievable precision. He captured first place in the 2006 Zurich Classic and carved his niche as a PGA Tour champion.

"This means so much," Couch said. "It's something from a

guy who came from nothing, and now I have a million dollars. It just goes to show you you're never out of it."

The story of Nehemiah in the Bible tells us that God is in the business of using unlikely people to rebuild things that are in ruins. Nehemiah was a common man who God asked to take on the task of rebuilding the wall of Jerusalem. You may not be assigned a job like Nehemiah was, but God sees immeasurable potential in you. He wants to rebuild His kingdom in your life! Even if things don't always go your way, take courage—and work hard for God's glory. You may be surprised what happens next.

—MOLLY RAMSEYER

PLAYING THROUGH

Have you ever felt that your potential has gone unnoticed? Take courage today—your Father in heaven will reward your hard work.

From the Guidebook: Read the story of Nehemiah (chapters 1–6).

NO. 67: CHAMPIONS GOLF CLUB, HOUSTON, TEXAS; CYPRESS CREEK COURSE

7,200 yards; built in 1959
Architect: Jack Burke Jr.
Host of US Open and Ryder Cup
www.championsgolfclub.com

68. WASN'T GOD WATCHING?

Approach Shot:
Understanding God's sovereignty

"Precious in the sight of the Lord is the death of his saints."
PSALM 116:15

When Payne Stewart boarded his final flight in October 1999, he was getting on a plane you would think God would spend a little extra time protecting. After all, this was not a group of boozing buddies sneaking off to a party. These were God-fearing, Jesus-loving people.

So what happened up there between earth and heaven that allowed Stewart and his fellow flyers to die? Did God look the other way? Was He not watching? Don't you get anything for trusting God? Why didn't He save those good people?

FAST FACT:
Payne Stewart won three majors in his career: the US Open in 1991 and 1999 and the PGA Championship in 1989.

If living on this earth were all there is to life, we'd be hopeless in answering those questions. But this is not all there is. Our time here is only a short prelude to an amazing eternal existence for those who know God through faith in Jesus Christ.

When it came time for Payne's eternal existence in heaven to begin, we saw things only from this side. We missed the remarkable homecoming Payne and his friends experienced when God ushered them into His presence, but we can imagine it was fantastic: "Precious in the sight of the Lord is the death of his saints" (Psalm 116:15).

That's small consolation. When death takes what matters most, it's not easy to say, "That's okay, God, we'll get along fine down here." But that's when we turn to Him and His promises. The same God who welcomes His children into heaven has promised to surround us with His arms of comfort. And He has promised never to leave us (Hebrews 13:5).

Was God watching? Yes, He was watching . . . and waiting with open arms. The same loving arms that on this side of heaven give us comfort.

—DAVE BRANON

PLAYING THROUGH

Have you had someone in your life taken from you through death? What were some of the things you have discussed with God concerning this event?

From the Guidebook: Read Psalm 23 for an incredible experience in comfort.

NO. 68: TORREY PINES GOLF CLUB, LA JOLLA, CALIFORNIA; SOUTH COURSE

Built in 1957
Architect: William F. Bell
Host of Buick Invitational; the course sits high above the
    Pacific Ocean shoreline
www.torreypinesgolfcourse.com

69. IMPERFECT BY DESIGN

*"I praise you because I am fearfully
and wonderfully made."*

PSALM 139:14

Have you ever noticed the dimples covering the surface of a golf ball? They make the ball look imperfect. So what's their purpose?

An aeronautical engineer who designs golf balls says that a perfectly smooth ball would travel only about 130 yards off the tee. But the same ball with the right kind of dimples will fly twice that far. These apparent "flaws" minimize the ball's air resistance and allow it to travel much farther.

FAST FACT:
The number of dimples on a golf ball varies from model to model. A ball generally has between 300 and 500 dimples. The average number is somewhere around 330.

Most of us can quickly name the physical characteristics we wish we had been born without. It's difficult to imagine that these "imperfections" are there for a purpose and are part of God's master design. Yet when the psalmist wrote of God's creative marvel in the womb, he said to the Lord, "You formed my inward parts" (Psalm 139:13 NKJV), and "Your eyes saw my unformed body" (v. 16). And he said, "I will praise you because I am fearfully and wonderfully made" (v. 14).

If we could accept our bodily "imperfections" as part of God's master plan for us, what a difference it would make in our outlook on life. The "dimples" we dislike may enable us

148

to bring the greatest glory to our wise and loving Creator, who knows how to get the best out of us.

—David McCasland

PLAYING THROUGH

Okay, let's do this: What physical characteristic do you like least about yourself? First, establish in your mind that God designed you just the way He wanted you. Second, tell God thank you for making you just as you are.

From the Guidebook: Read Psalm 139:13–18.

NO. 69: PGA WEST, LA QUINTA, CALIFORNIA; STADIUM COURSE

7,300 yards; built in 1986
Architect: Pete Dye
Home of the PGA Tour Q-School finals on alternate years; location of famed "Alcatraz" (hole no. 17)
www.pgawest.com

70. STANDING ON SHOULDERS

Approach Shot:
Observing and gleaning from others

"How can we thank God enough for you in return for all the joy we have in the presence of your God because of you?"

1 THESSALONIANS 3:9

In the early days of pro golf, women were not considered professionals. There were no professional events for women, and most country clubs did not allow women to play as members. In 1946 there were enough pro women to form a league and hold their first ever US Women's Open. Ladies like Patty Berg, Betty Jameson, Louise Suggs, and Babe Zaharias were among those who broke the gender barrier—eventually allowing for the young brilliant rookies to compete today in the modern-day US Women's Open. Current young stars such as Paula Creamer, Lorena Ochoa, and Natalie Gulbis stand on the shoulders of those who have gone before them.

FAST FACT:
The US Women's Amateur was first played in 1895, 58 years before the current tournament was sanctioned by the USGA.

The 2005 Women's Open took place at Cherry Hills Country Club, which just happens to be outside the back door of my house. Thousands of people came in droves to witness new talent, breathtaking accuracy, and the thrill of competition. And I'm sure some fans were on the shoulders of others trying to catch a glance of the unfolding history of women's pro golf.

Are there people in your past who have allowed you to experience the success you have today? Trained by Moses, Joshua would later become the leader who would deliver God's people into the Promised Land. Although Moses did not get to see the Promised Land himself, Joshua stood on his shoulders. The Bible is full of forerunners, people God sends ahead to pave the way.

Whose shoulders do you stand on?

—Molly Ramseyer

PLAYING THROUGH

When was the last time you expressed your thankfulness to those who have gone before you—those who have paved the way for you? Commit to do that today.

From the Guidebook: Read Numbers 27:22–23. By whom do you feel you've been commissioned? Who has "sent you out?"

NO. 70: CHERRY HILLS COUNTRY CLUB, ENGLEWOOD, COLORADO; CHERRY HILLS COURSE

7,160 yards; built in 1923
Architect: William S. Flynn
Host of two PGA Championships and the 2005 US
   Women's Open
www.chcc.com

71. CLOSE CALLS

*"This is the word of the Lord to Zerubbabel:
'Not by might nor by power, but by my Spirit,'
says the Lord Almighty."*

ZECHARIAH 4:6

Young Australian PGA Tour golfer Aaron Baddeley took a one-shot lead over world No. 1-ranked Tiger Woods in the final round of the 2007 US Open at Oakmont Golf Club outside of Pittsburgh.

Thirteen years earlier, Christian golfer Loren Roberts, known as the Boss of the Putting Moss for his putting skill, lined up an uphill, 5-foot putt at the same Oakmont course to clinch a win over Ernie Els at the 1994 US Open.

FAST FACT:
Baddeley was the youngest-ever winner of the Australian Open at age 19 and has multiple wins on the PGA Tour.

Both men, separated in age and background but united in their faith in Jesus Christ and their desire to follow Him, wanted to perform at their very best and to claim an earthly honor that could be used to God's glory.

However, both golfers fell short. Baddeley made a triple bogey 7 on the par 4 first hole to fall out of the lead. He endured a long day, which dropped him far back on the US Open leaderboard.

Roberts missed his putt just barely to the right and watched as Els later captured the first of his two US Open titles.

"I had a 5-foot putt to win the US Open. That's every golfer's dream, and I missed it," Roberts recalled.

But neither man let the earthly disappointments of this world deter him from his spiritual purpose and witness. "The verse that kept coming to mind that day was 1 Peter 5:5, 'God opposes the proud but gives grace to the humble,'" Baddeley said. "God was using me for His purpose."

Roberts never won a US Open but has remained steadfast in the Tour Bible study and became a star on the Champions Tour. Baddeley shares his testimony nationwide with audiences on how faith in God can help overcome disappointment.

That's something every person—inside or outside of golf—can use in life.

—ART STRICKLIN

PLAYING THROUGH

What disappointments at work or at home have you suffered? How did you handle them?

From the Guidebook: Read 1 Peter 5.

NO. 71: GOZZER RANCH COUNTRY CLUB, COEUR D'ALENE, IDAHO

> 7,143 yards; built in 2007
> Architect: Tom Fazio
> Lakes, mountains, forests provide remarkable vistas
> www.gozzerranchclub.com

72. SWING MUSIC

"Continue to live in him."
COLOSSIANS 2:6

In golf, it helps to watch top players swing the golf club. I think if I devoted enough time to observing the truly great players, my golf game would dramatically improve. Once I envision what a good swing looks like, it gives me a new perspective when I look at my own swing.

But there is more to it than watching. One famous golf coach said there is really no secret to his most successful students' success. He says the best players, for the most part, work on the same things over and over again. He said that even his very best player would slip back into bad habits if he was not continually working on the fundamentals of his swing.

Just like top golfers have certain tendencies in their swing that, if left unchecked, can become a problem, so does each of us have a tendency to sin—and that will result in disaster.

Our desire and vision for Christlike living should not be focused on our own "swing." Instead it must be focused on Jesus Christ, who is perfect in every way. Paul told us, "Just as you received Christ Jesus as Lord, continue to live in him, rooted and built up in him" (Colossians 2:6). Our imitation of Jesus is not merely found in outward acts of kindness and mercy, but it is first an inward attitude of

FAST FACT:

After spending 14 years as an NFL quarterback, Reich served for a time as president of Reformed Theological Seminary in Charlotte, North Carolina.

humility toward God—which brings confidence, peace, and hope that the "world" does not know.

Tiger is continually working on his swing. In the same way we would do well to pursue with the same intensity a continual improvement of our relationship with Jesus Christ.

—FRANK REICH

PLAYING THROUGH

Write down three steps you would like to take to enhance your relationship with Jesus Christ.

From the Guidebook: Read Colossians 2:6–12.

NO. 72: WHISTLING STRAITS, SHEBOYGAN, WISCONSIN; IRISH COURSE

7,201 yards; built in 2000

Architect: Pete Dye

Just inland from Lake Michigan, the Irish Course is marked by creeks, grasslands, and dunes

www.destinationkohler.com

73. THE ENCOURAGER

*"May the God of hope fill you with all joy and peace
as you trust in him, so that you may overflow
with hope by the power of the Holy Spirit."*

ROMANS 15:13

I had one of the most disappointing years of my career in 2003. I had made four cuts in 14 tournaments, and for the first time in my golf career, I was in the red financially.

Times like that make me question whether I should stay the course as an LPGA player. I wondered if all the hard work I had done over the years was really paying off, or if I had just hit my peak. Thoughts of giving up were there.

FAST FACT:

Born in Malaysia, Siew Ai Lim came to the United States to attend the University of South Carolina.

Fortunately for me, I had a tremendous coach who continued to encourage me to keep persevering. He saw my potential and knew that I had so much more inside of me to become one of the top players on Tour. His encouragement and my continued perseverance in working on my game paid off as I had one of my most successful seasons on the LPGA Tour in 2004.

Looking back, I see how that parallels with my spiritual life. There are times when I feel like I'm getting nowhere in my spiritual journey, and I feel beaten down. I wonder if the difficulties I face in life are worth the effort I'm putting in as a Christian and a follower of Christ.

When we feel that way, the good news is that all of us as followers of Christ have an Encourager, the Holy Spirit. He's the still, quiet voice that tells us to keep going. He's the one who says we have so much more to achieve if only we stay the course. Listen to the Encourager. Persevere and keep pressing on to the finish line.

—SIEW AI LIM

PLAYING THROUGH

What is discouraging you right now? How much time have you spent talking to the Lord about it—and then listening to the Holy Spirit's encouraging guidance?

From the Guidebook: Memorize Romans 15:13.

NO. 73: THE QUARRY GOLF COURSE, SAN ANTONIO, TEXAS

6,740 yards; built in 1993
Architect: Keith Foster
Built on the site of an abandoned stone quarry
www.quarrygolf.com

74. "HE DIDN'T EVEN MENTION RELIGION"

*"Have nothing to do with the fruitless deeds
of darkness, but rather expose them."*

EPHESIANS 5:11

In his powerful book *The Holiness of God*, R. C. Sproul observed that unbelievers often feel uneasy in the presence of an obedient Christian. The holiness of God reflected in a believer's life makes the non-Christian uncomfortable. Sproul then told the following true incident to illustrate his point.

A well-known professional golfer was playing in a tournament with President Gerald Ford, fellow pro Jack Nicklaus, and Billy Graham. After the round was over, one of the other pros on the PGA Tour asked, "Hey, what was it like playing with the President and Billy Graham?" The pro said with disgust, "I don't need Billy Graham stuffing religion down my throat!" With that he headed for the practice tee. His friend followed, and after the angry golfer had pounded out his fury on a bucket of golf balls, his fellow golfer asked, "Was Billy a little rough on you out there?" The pro sighed and said with embarrassment, "No, he didn't even mention religion."

FAST FACT:
According to legend, Billy Graham once said, "The Lord answers my prayers everywhere except on the course."

Sproul commented, "Astonishingly, Billy Graham had said nothing about God, Jesus, or religion, yet the pro stomped away after the game accusing Billy of trying to ram religion down his throat." What had happened? Simply this: The evangelist had so reflected Christlikeness that his presence made the pro feel uncomfortable.

I wonder, do unbelievers sense our godly influence? If we are identified with Christ and walk in holiness, they will—before we even mention religion.

—DAVE EGNER

PLAYING THROUGH

What are three characteristics of your life that you think could attract people to Jesus? What can you improve in your life to make yourself more Christlike?

From the Guidebook: Read Ephesians 5:8–16.

NO. 74: CONGRESSIONAL COUNTRY CLUB, BETHESDA, MARYLAND; BLUE COURSE

7,245 yards; built in 1924

Architect: Devereux Emmet; renovated by Rees Jones in 1989

Host of three US Opens, the PGA Championship, and the US Senior Open

www.ccclub.org

75. WALK WITH THE WISE

"He who walks with the wise grows wise."
PROVERBS 13:20

LPGA golfer Tracy Hanson chooses to spend the majority of her time with people who encourage her to stay true to her Christian beliefs. She avoids close friendships with people who tempt her to do things she knows are wrong.

College friends and her friends on the LPGA Tour have walked with Tracy through the hard and fun times in life. But most important, they have helped her grow in her Christian faith. Tracy's faith has taught her that her worth is from Jesus Christ—and only Him—not from how she performs on the golf course.

FAST FACT:

Tracy enjoys speaking at Fellowship of Christian Athletes functions. Find out more at www.tracyhanson. com

"Recognizing Jesus Christ as the source of my true value has helped stabilize my emotions and has given me a bigger perspective of what life is all about," Tracy says. "It's not just about golf and what I do on the golf course. It's about relating with Christ and with people."

"Fortunately, on Tour I was able to get together with other Christian women. We met weekly for Bible study, fellowship, and prayer. I am grateful for these relationships and for older mentors who show how to stay strong in the Lord and to experience His grace and comfort in good and difficult times."

Tracy knows that "He who walks with the wise grows wise, but a companion of fools suffers harm" (Proverbs 13:20).

Whether she's at home in Michigan where she now lives now that she as retired from the LPGA or out on a Pro-Am appearance, Tracy looks to God for wisdom to know who she should spend time with.

What a great example! We each need to recognize the impact other people have on our choices and the way we view ourselves. That will help us choose friends who lead us closer to God, not farther from Him.

—Roxanne Robbins

PLAYING THROUGH

What kind of messages do your friends send you about your value to God? Today, thank a friend or mentor who has helped you better understand God's deep love for you.

From the Guidebook: Read Titus 2:1–8.

NO. 75: NANEA GOLF CLUB, KAILUA-KONA, HAWAII

7,503 yards; built in 2002

Architect: David McLay Kidd

One of the most exclusive courses in the world; every hole has views of the Pacific Ocean

76. GOD'S GOT A PLAN

" 'For I know the plans I have for you,'
declares the Lord. 'Plans to prosper you.' "
JEREMIAH 29:11

My last week playing as an amateur included some of the worst golf I'd ever played in my life, and I seriously doubted whether "turning pro" and going onto the Futures Tour (equivalent to a minor league) was the best thing for me. After a lot of prayer and discussion with family and close friends, I felt the urge to simply pack my bags and see what would happen.

FAST FACT:

Katherine was the 2003 NCAA Player of the Year while attending Pepperdine University.

Fortunately, God had bigger plans than I anticipated, and I ended up winning my first and second tournament as a professional on the Futures Tour. After earning "Non-exempt" status for the 2004 LPGA season, I was again unsure of where I was meant to be playing. After more prayer and deliberation I made the choice to play the LPGA for three months. However, after nine weeks of failing to pre-qualify for tournaments and no paychecks, I started to think God wanted me to play the Futures Tour instead. Upon realizing I had missed the entry deadline for five Futures Tour events, I had no choice but to stick to the LPGA.

Little did I know that God would yet again bless me beyond expectation and lead me to finish 69th on the 2004 money list, high enough to keep full eligibility for the 2005 season.

When I reflect on my first two years as a professional, I realize that God was not only teaching me patience and perseverance but he was also teaching me trust in His "plans to prosper" me and give me "hope and a future."

—Katherine Hull

PLAYING THROUGH

Are you striving at something you are sure God wants you to do but you are failing? How can you know when it is time to stop going and begin something new?

From the Guidebook: Read Psalm 40:1–5.

NO. 76: CHAMPIONS HILL GOLF CLUB, HENDERSONVILLE, NORTH CAROLINA

6,676 yards; built in 1990
Architect: Tom Fazio
Set in the Blue Ridge Mountains, it is the home course of
   designer Tom Fazio
www.championhills.com

77. GOD'S HALL OF FAME

*"For God so loved the world that he gave his
one and only Son, that whoever believes in him
shall not perish but have eternal life."*

JOHN 3:16

In golf, as in most other professional sports, the highest honor any player can achieve is induction into the Hall of Fame.

In golf, several organizations came together several years ago to form the World Golf Hall of Fame near Jacksonville, Florida. Each fall, the greatest in the game gather at the World Golf Hall of Fame to honor the latest inductees in nationally televised ceremonies.

FAST FACT:
Texas has more players than any other state in the World Golf Hall of Fame. California is second.

The game's greatest players—from Byron Nelson and Ben Hogan to Lee Trevino and Jack Nicklaus—have all been inducted. The players elected must be named on a certain number of ballots returned from a variety of golf experts. If players aren't named on enough ballots, they can't be inducted regardless of how many tournaments they won during their career.

God has a Hall of Fame of sorts—a Hall of Honor for His special people.

But unlike golf's version, there is not a wide number of experts that decides who gets in after achieving a certain number of votes. God is the ultimate judge, and He opens His Hall of Honor—also known as heaven—to anyone who accepts His Son, Jesus Christ, as Savior.

There is no annual induction for the newest members, but instant acceptance happens whenever someone accepts Christ into his or her life. Induction comes when the believer is ushered into God's glorious heaven.

Golf Hall of Fame inductees are given just 12 minutes during induction ceremonies to thank everyone who helped them in their careers. Christians will have eternity to sing God's praises and thank Jesus for what He did on the cross.

Are you in the Hall?

—ART STRICKLIN

PLAYING THROUGH

Are you in God's Hall of Fame? Do you know you can have instant acceptance? Do you need to talk to someone about this?

From the Guidebook: Read the book of Romans and discover God's road to salvation.

NO. 77: INVERNESS CLUB, TOLEDO, OHIO
7,300 yards; built in 1919
Architect: Donald Ross
Host of four US Opens and two PGA Championship tournaments; Byron Nelson at one time served as the golf professional at Inverness
www.invernessclub.com

78. TEES AND TREES

*"But the fruit of the Spirit is love, joy, peace,
patience, kindness, goodness, faithfulness,
gentleness, and self-control."*

GALATIANS 5:22–23

My buddy took a swing with his golf club, and the ball careened to the left and headed for the trees. It was one ugly shot from the fairway of the Thousand Oaks golf course.

As the ball sailed through the air, all eyes were on its final destination—deep in the trees. It struck one oak hard, ricocheted off a few others, and bounded out of sight.

Now, some people would have lost their self-control at this point. They would have kicked the turf, broken their two-iron in two, or communicated things that shouldn't be stated—or thought, for that matter.

However, my buddy simply smiled and said, "Well, it looks like they're going to have to rename this place 999 Oaks."

Whether you're playing golf or participating in any other activity where failure is possible, it pays to maintain your self-control. One great way to do this is to avoid taking yourself too seriously. My friend's use of humor helped him cope with his disappointment.

When you're filled with the Holy Spirit, you can experience self-control along with "love, joy, peace, patience, kindness, goodness, faithfulness, [and] gentleness"

FAST FACT:
Golf club manufacturers say that nearly one-quarter of all broken clubs returned for replacement were damaged by golfer abuse.

(Galatians 5:22–23). And you can see with a fresh perspective that the proper response to life's errant shots is the godly way.

Instead of getting upset and losing control when things don't go your way, pray and ask God to fill you with His Spirit. With His guidance and assistance, you can stay in control and demonstrate to those around you the reality of your faith.

It sure beats breaking a nine-iron over your knee.

—TOM FELTEN

PLAYING THROUGH

When things don't go well today and you feel yourself being filled with things far from the fruit of the Spirit, confess it to God and pray, "Lord, fill me with Your Spirit." Move forward with a renewed perspective.

From the Guidebook: Read Galatians 5:13–26.

NO. 78: THE FARM, ROCKY FACE, GEORGIA

6,906 yards; built in 1988

Architect: Tom Fazio

Home of the Carpet Capital Invitational Collegiate Golf Tournament

www.thefarmgolfclub.org

79. MOVING GOD'S HEART

"So let us come boldly to the throne of our gracious God."
HEBREWS 4:16 (NLT)

Mattie Stepanek died at the young age of 13 from a rare form of muscular dystrophy. Mattie lived his short life more joyfully than someone who had just won the Masters. Why? He had perspective. Most of us would ask, "Why me?" Not Mattie. He asked, "Why not me?" God looks very carefully at how we handle tough times.

Someone else who never asked the question, "Why me?" was my pastor and mentor Ron Mehl. Pastor Ron died a few years ago of leukemia, which he fought for 22 years. Because of God's promises and faithfulness, Ron was also able to live a joyful life in spite of the difficult and sometimes painful circumstances.

FAST FACT:

One of Ben Crane's characteristics as a golfer is that he plays the game slowly and deliberately.

In his book *A Prayer That Moves Heaven*, Pastor Ron wrote, "Life is unpredictable. Challenges are unavoidable. I see this verse [Hebrews 4:16] urging us to come boldly again and again to the throne of grace, keeping our mercy-and-grace tank full, because we never know when we will need it. I want to live at His throne of mercy and grace. I want to pitch my tent and set up camp right there."

Romans 5:3 teaches us that we should consider it pure joy when we face trials of any kind, because these trials produce endurance. Our times of dwelling at His throne make it possible for us to face these trials with joy. When I am challenged or in the midst of difficult times, I remind myself that if I am not able to come to God when things aren't going my way, how can I expect God to want to bless me?

With golf, the highs are high and the lows are low. I know that if I can be faithful in the lows, God will be able to trust me with the highs.

—BEN CRANE

PLAYING THROUGH

Can you look back at a tough time and see any good that came from it? Can you think of a specific challenge that God used to draw you closer to Him?

From the Guidebook: Read Hebrews 4.

NO. 79: MAIDSTONE CLUB, EAST HAMPTON, NEW YORK

6,423 yards; built in 1891

Architect: William Tucker

Golfers interact with tidal marshes, sand dunes, and the Atlantic Ocean

80. GOD CARES ABOUT THE SMALL THINGS

"I thank my God every time I remember you."
PHILIPPIANS 1:3

It was Saturday afternoon, and I just hung up the phone with Mom. I asked her to tell me she loved me, something I had never had to do before. But something in my spirit prompted me to make sure I heard her say, "I love you, Honey."

Mom was in her ninth month of battling melanoma cancer, and her body was wearing out rapidly. I called home every day to talk with her. As the days passed, the conversations became shorter and shorter.

FAST FACT:
Tracy enjoys spending her summer downtime on the beaches of Lake Michigan.

The day after my perplexing conversation, I received a call from home. It was my sister telling me that mom had died a few hours earlier. I was stunned, speechless, and paralyzed.

In my state of shock, I thought back to that conversation the day prior. God knew I needed to hear those words one more time. He created a memory that I can hold on to during the times when I miss mom and I long to pick up the phone and just say, "Hello."

It's easy to forget to thank God for the blessings He's given me in my life. But the one gift I will continue to thank Him for is the remembrance of my mother's last words to me.

Remember to "Devote yourselves to prayer, being watchful and thankful" (Colossians 4:2). And thank God for the small things.

—TRACY HANSON

PLAYING THROUGH

Write down five things you are thankful for this past week. Spend time in prayer talking to God and thanking Him for these blessings.

From the Guidebook: Read Psalm 136 and notice the many things we have to praise God for.

NO. 80: EAGLE VAIL GOLF CLUB, AVON, COLORADO

6,819 yards; built in 1974

Architects: Bruce Devlin and Robert von Hagge

A mountain course populated by aspens, lodgepole pines, and firs

www.eaglevailgolfclub.com

81. CAN YOU OUTGIVE GOD?

Approach Shot:
Honoring God with your resources

"Bring the whole tithe into the storehouse."
MALACHI 3:10

In my first year as a professional golfer, my church voiced a concern for a family that urgently needed financial help. I felt a nudging to contribute to the benevolent fund, but I was unsure of the amount I should commit. After some thought and prayer, I decided I would give 10 percent of my next tournament check to the fund on top of my regular tithe. Considering that my biggest check in my professional career until then was $2,000, I didn't think much of it.

FAST FACT:
Siew Ai Lim was an All-American golfer and the SEC Player of the Year in 1995 at the University of South Carolina.

In the very next tournament I played, I finished tied for second place and took home the biggest check of my career—$4,000. Now I was in a little bit of a dilemma. I was expecting to give around $200 to this fund, but now 10 percent would mean I would have to double that.

To make my decision even more difficult, I had not told anyone about my vow. Furthermore, I was sure that whatever I did contribute would have been received with thanksgiving. I decided to write the check for $400 and send it off immediately—before I could have second thoughts. As I was leaving for the next tournament, the family I was staying with for the week put a card in my car just before I pulled out.

Once I arrived at my next destination, I opened the card and found $500 in cash along with several prepaid calling cards. They had no idea of my commitment to God, but God knew.

You can never outgive God. This does not mean that in order for God to bless you, you have to give money to the church. It's not about us—it's about Him. He wants us to be faithful in the stewardship of the resources He gives us—and to honor our commitments.

—Siew Ai Lim

PLAYING THROUGH

What about this idea of tithing? Is it a habit in your life? Could it be possible that it is the least God expects of us?

From the Guidebook: Read Leviticus 27 and Malachi 3, and consider how those Old Testament standards should fit into your world today.

NO. 81: SCIOTO COUNTRY CLUB, COLUMBUS, OHIO

6,955 yards; built in 1915

Architect: Donald J. Ross

The course that built Jack—it was where Jack Nicklaus learned the game as a kid; host of each of these tournaments: US Open, PGA Championship, Ryder Cup, US Senior Open Championship, and US Amateur Championship

www.sciotocc.com

82. THE POWER OF THE WORD

Approach Shot:
Leaning on God's power

"All Scripture is God-breathed and is useful for teaching."
2 TIMOTHY 3:16

I can remember stepping onto the 17th hole at Tournament Players Club at Sawgrass in Florida. All I could see was the large lake surrounding the green. It looked like the Atlantic Ocean! I began to feel anxious and fearful, and I thought to myself, "You don't want to make a mistake here!"

I've had other "large lakes" in my life—not just on the golf course—and I've discovered that God has given me a resource which, when followed, will keep me from making wrong choices and devastating mistakes. That resource is called the Bible.

FAST FACT:
Ben Crane's first two PGA wins were Milwaukee's US Bank Championship in 2005 and the Duluth, Georgia, BellSouth Classic in 2003.

One way I am able to focus on God's Word when I am playing a tournament is by writing down a Scripture verse and placing it in the front of my yardage guidebook. Every time I see that verse, I know I can depend on God to carry out His will for my life.

Depending on God's Word will help me keep my eyes on Him and trust His promises and His love. Scripture will keep me from being consumed with fear. What a freeing feeling when I can stand up to any shot or over any putt or any other problem and know that this is all for God's glory and not my own!

What are the "large lakes" in your life? Do you desire to have God do extraordinary things through you? God tells us in His Word that He has made His power available to all of us alike. And it comes through knowing and understanding His power and His Word.

—Ben Crane

PLAYING THROUGH

Ben Crane says that his success on the PGA Tour might surprise some. He says he was "by no means a standout" as an amateur. But he "gave God my best, worked hard, and was available to God." He says he knows that God had His touch on his life because that's what God's Word tells him. What are some important things God's Word is telling you?

From the Guidebook: Read Psalm 119:105–112.

NO. 82: TPC SAWGRASS, PONTE VEDRA BEACH, FLORIDA; STADIUM COURSE

    6,954 yards; built in 1981; renovated in 2006
    Architect: Pete Dye
    Home of the famous No. 17 island green; host of the PGA
        Players Championship
    www.tpc.com/sawgrass

83. WHAT DISADVANTAGE?

"[Jesus] replied, . . . 'Nothing will be impossible for you.'"
MATTHEW 17:20

Golf is a game of precision, timing, balance, and mental fortitude. It takes every part of your body working together to play this game well—or does it?

In the year 2000, a group of one-armed golfers formed the North American One-Armed Golfer Association. Most people stare at them and wonder how in the world they can play with such a glaring disadvantage, but they don't always see it that way. Steve Quevillion, who won the 2006 one-armed title and tied for third in 2010, said, "On chips, I see so many guys move their second hand all over the place, but we can just let the club do the work." It's amazing what these men have accomplished.

FAST FACT:

Good one-armed golfers consistently drive the ball 280 yards or more.

In Matthew 17 the disciples came to Jesus feeling disadvantaged and asking why they didn't have the power to drive out demons. Jesus replied by saying, "Because you have so little faith. I tell you the truth, if you have faith as small as a mustard seed, you can say to this mountain, 'Move from here to there' and it will move. Nothing will be impossible for you" (Matthew 17:20–21).

Is there something in your life that puts you at a disadvantage? Have you believed that it is impossible to overcome? Like children who have only begun to walk, most of us have only begun our faith adventure. Jesus reminds us that no matter what kind of handicap we may face, just a small amount of faith can help us overcome the impossible.

—MOLLY RAMSEYER

PLAYING THROUGH

Why is it hard to believe that with God all things are possible? What is one thing in your life that has made you believe that God can do the impossible?

From the Guidebook: Read Matthew 19:26, Mark 10:27, and Luke 1:37.

NO. 83: ARONIMINK GOLF CLUB, NEWTOWN SQUARE, PENNSYLVANIA

Built in 1929

Architect: Donald J. Ross

Ross designed over 600 courses, but he called this one "my masterpiece"; host of both the PGA Championship and Senior PGA Championship

www.aronimink.org

84. FORE!-GETFUL

"Be careful that you do not forget the Lord your God."

DEUTERONOMY 8:11

Do you have a personal sports moment you can't forget? Was it the time you finally beat Uncle Rufus in croquet? Ah, yes, the success and joy lingers in your mind as one sweet memory!

That's what makes the following news story so sad. A 50-year-old golfer from Taiwan was playing 18 with some friends in Xinsu City. He hit a beautiful drive on a par 3 that ended up rolling right into the cup—a hole in one!

As his friends ran up to congratulate him, the man was muttering to himself and asking, "Why am I here?" They took him to a hospital and doctors diagnosed him with having temporary memory loss. After some rest, he began to lose much of his amnesia. But a week later he still couldn't remember hitting that ace.

FAST FACT:
The possibility of an average golfer making a hole-in-one is approximately 12,700 to 1!

God spoke through Moses to tell His people a few things about not being forgetful. They had come through a grueling 40-year trip in the wilderness. But it was nearing the time for them to enter the Promised Land. Moses said, "Be careful that you do not forget the Lord your God, failing to observe his commands" (v. 11).

It would be easy for these people to forget God in their new "milk and honey" place in the world. Newfound prosperity and blessing could lead to pride . . . and forgetfulness. God knew that their hearts could "become proud" (v. 14)—full of themselves but devoid of praise and thanks to Himself. So He warned them—and *us*.

Has your recent success caused you to forget God? How have you responded to blessing—with gratitude or forgetfulness?

—TOM FELTEN

PLAYING THROUGH

Jot down two or three big blessings that have come your way recently. Spend a few minutes in prayer thanking God for His provision in your life.

From the Guidebook: Read Deuteronomy 8:11–18.

NO. 84: BLACKWOLF RUN GOLF COURSE, KOHLER, WISCONSIN; RIVER COURSE

6,991 yards; built in 2002

Architect: Pete Dye

Designed to test the accuracy of golfers, the River Course has been called, "the nation's finest public-access course" by *GOLF Magazine*

www.destinationkohler.com

85. TAKE ACTION

Approach Shot:
Showing your faith by your works

"What good is it, my brothers, if a man claims to have faith but has no deeds?"

JAMES 2:14

In order to win any game, match, or race, one cannot simply rely on faith. In addition to a belief in being able to win, the player must also take action by executing a game plan.

Salvation is similar. While we cannot "win" or "earn" our salvation, God's amazing gift of grace and mercy does require us to respond and "take action." Notice what James said. "In the same way, faith by itself, if it is not accompanied by action, is dead . . . You see that his faith and his actions were working together, and his faith was made complete by what he did . . . You see that a person is justified by what he does and not by faith alone" (James 2:17, 22, 24).

FAST FACT:

While at Pepperdine, Katherine Hull recorded the lowest 18-hole total in NCAA history.

The responsibility and "game plan" of every Christian should be to make Christ known throughout the world. Matthew 28:19 tells us to "go and make disciples of all nations," and 2 Corinthians 5:20 says we are "Christ's ambassadors." Although we may have doubts in our ability to proclaim the good news, we need to remember that God will enable the Holy Spirit to work through us in order to fulfill His plan.

Moses did not think he was capable of leading the Israelites out of Egypt, but he finally trusted God to enable Him. The Bible frequently tells us that salvation is a gift from God, and we are saved by His grace alone. But Scripture also tells us to take action.

What is your game plan for the works that show your faith? (See 2 Corinthians 12:9; Romans 3:23; Ephesians 2:8; Titus 3:3–7; Galatians 2:21.)

—Katherine Hull

PLAYING THROUGH

What deeds do you think God wants you to do as a demonstration of your faith? Do you have a "game plan" for putting your faith into action?

From the Guidebook: Read James 2.

NO. 85: SAHALEE COUNTRY CLUB, SAMMAMISH, WASHINGTON

6,931 yards; built in 1969
Architect: Ted Robinson
Host of the 1998 PGA Championship and the 2010 US
   Senior Open
www.sahalee.com

86. BACKYARD TEE SHOT

Approach Shot:
Enjoying Christ's forgiveness

"Christ's love compels us."
2 CORINTHIANS 5:14

I read a story some time ago about an aspiring young golfer who spent hours in his backyard practicing his golf swing. He wasn't allowed to use a real golf ball close to the house, only a plastic practice ball.

One day, when he thought both his parents were gone, he longed to hear the sweet click of a club head meeting a real golf ball. So he went outside, teed one up, took a mighty swing, and accidentally hit the ball through his parents' bedroom window.

FAST FACT:
Some companies specialize in building backyard putting greens.

I'll let him tell the rest of the story: "I heard the glass shatter, and then I heard my mother cry out. I ran into the house and up the stairs to her bedroom. She was standing there in front of the broken window and she was bleeding. I started to cry and I couldn't stop. All I could say was 'Mom, what have I done! What have I done! I'm so sorry! I'm so sorry!' Her response was to hug me and say, 'It's all right; everything's going to be all right.' After that I never wanted to take a real golf ball in the backyard."

When we think about our Lord's suffering for us on the cross, we should want to live "for him who died for [us] and was raised again" (2 Corinthians 5:15). After we've heard His words of forgiveness, there are things we just never want to do again—in the backyard, or in any other place.

—DAVID ROPER

PLAYING THROUGH

What have you done recently for which you have yet to ask forgiveness? Is it time to stop and ask God to put His arms of love around you and remind you of His forgiving love?

From the Guidebook: Read 2 Corinthians 5:9–15.

NO. 86: PUMPKIN RIDGE GOLF COURSE, NORTH PLAINS, OREGON; GHOST CREEK COURSE

6,839 yards; built in 1991
Architect: Robert Cupp
Host of 1993 and 1994 Nike Tour Championships
www.pumpkinridge.com

87. GOD'S MONEY LIST

"For the love of money is a root of all kinds of evil. Some people, eager for money, have wandered from the faith and pierced themselves with many griefs."

1 TIMOTHY 6:10

The game of golf is unique in many ways, but none more so than the weekly money list printed for all to see.

Unlike just about every other professional sport you can think of—or just about any other profession for that matter—the weekly earnings for every golfer are printed in weekly newspapers and golf magazines following each tournament.

FAST FACT:

Paul Stankowski, who has career earnings of more than $6 million, contributes heavily to Christian causes.

The money generated from the PGA Tour can be quite good indeed for the winners. In one recent year, more than 100 players made at least one million dollars playing professional golf. An additional 50 made a half-million.

But in relation to what the Bible says about the love of money, how should Christians react to earning a large income? Christian PGA Tour golfer Paul Stankowski, who has made several million, has good advice for players in the game of golf and the game of life.

"If I want to go out and buy a BMW because it's a BMW and people would see me in it—that's a problem. But if I can afford it and I'm not neglecting something else that could use the money, then why not do it?

"The key issue is this: Why are you doing something? Why are you buying a house? Why are you buying a car? Why are you buying clothes? Why are you doing this or that? It can be a struggle. If all you want to do is show off, then that is materialism."

You may never earn a cent on the golf course but earn your money elsewhere. Remember to keep in perspective the One who makes all things possible.

—ART STRICKLIN

PLAYING THROUGH

Examine your income, possessions, and lifestyle. Are they in line with proper God-honoring goals or more worldly materialism?

For Further Study: Read *Money, Possessions & Eternity* by Randy Alcorn.

NO. 87: COEUR D'ALENE GOLF COURSE, COEUR D'ALENE, IDAHO

    6,803 yards; built in 1991

    Architect: Scott Miller

    Unusual feature: Hole 14 is floating in Lake Coeur d'Alene,
        and golfers have to take a boat to get to it.

    www.cdaresort.com/golf

88. UNLIKELY HEROES

*"God chose the foolish things of the world
to shame the wise."*

1 CORINTHIANS 1:27

Something deep inside all of us delights when an underdog wins an impossible battle.

How did you feel after watching the movie *The Rookie*, *Hoosiers*, *The Mighty Ducks*, *Rocky*, *Rudy*, or *The Greatest Game Ever Played*? This golf drama is based on the true story of the 1913 US Open, in which 20-year-old amateur Francis Quimet defeats reigning champion Harry Vardon. It's the age-old plot of the most unlikely athlete winning it all, and yet something inside of me leapt for joy at his moment of victory!

The Bible contains the same kinds of stories, underdogs who succeed at unlikely events. Look at the account of David and Goliath (1 Samuel 17) or Joseph when he was sold into slavery (Genesis 37) or Joshua when he marched around the walls of Jericho (Joshua 6). But the most central of all underdogs in history was Jesus Christ. Talk about an unlikely hero!

I believe that God made something deep inside all of us delight when an underdog wins an impossible battle. In lots of ways, God is communicating with us that He chooses "the foolish things of the world to shame the wise"(1 Corinthians

1:27). God is not finished working out His will in history, and the Bible account isn't the end of His work.

He is still using unlikely heroes today! Will you be one?

—MOLLY RAMSEYER

PLAYING THROUGH

Do you believe God can use even you to shame the wise? Pray today and ask for a greater measure of faith.

From the Guidebook: Read all three biblical accounts mentioned above: Genesis 37, Joshua 6, and 1 Samuel 17.

NO. 88: HARBOUR TOWN GOLF LINKS, HILTON HEAD, SOUTH CAROLINA

6,973 yards; built in 1966

Architect: Pete Dye

Host of the Verizon Heritage each year

www.seapines.com

89. CAPTIVE THOUGHTS

Approach Shot:
Controlling what you think about

*"Your servant will meditate on your decrees. Your statutes
are my delight; they are my counselors."*

PSALM 119:23–24

What are you thinking about?

Yeah, now. What are you thinking about right now?

Experts have a fancy name for thinking about thinking.
They call it *metacognition*. It's not something we normally
engage in. Normally, we just think—with no
thinking about it.

FAST FACT:

Jeff Hopper is editor of Links Letter, *a golf magazine that can be accessed at www.linksplayers.com.*

But when those experts play in the realm of
sports, they challenge athletes to be far more
intentional about their thoughts. And with golf
being the "thinking man's game," that inten-
tionality is pushed to the nth degree—whether
or not you're a man! The spiritual life belongs
to thinking men and women too.

Those who meditate on God's law day and night are called
blessed, made fruitful in all they do (Psalm 1).

Those who give their lives to Christ renew their minds,
becoming people of heaven rather than people of earth
(Romans 12:2).

Those who follow Him take every thought captive to make
it obedient to Christ (2 Corinthians 10:5).

And those seeking the righteousness of Christ turn their
minds to "whatever is true, whatever is noble, whatever is
right, whatever is pure, whatever is lovely, whatever is admi-

rable"—if anything is excellent or praiseworthy (Philippians 4:8).

So let's ask it again: What are you thinking about right now?

—Jeff Hopper

PLAYING THROUGH

How captive is your thinking? How can you corral it in so that each time your thoughts drift outside of Philippians 4:8, you turn back to godly thinking?

From the Guidebook: Read Philippians 4.

NO. 89: LONG POINT GOLF COURSE, AMELIA ISLAND, FLORIDA

6,775 yards; built in 1987

Architect: Tom Fazio

Located on Amelia Island, which is northeast of Jacksonville, this course has hosted the US Open

www.aipfl.com/golf/longpoint.htm

90. WEEKEND DUFFER?

Approach Shot:
Exercising spiritually

"Exercise yourself toward godliness."
1 TIMOTHY 4:7 (NKJV)

Good morning! Only one more day until Friday!" Our local traffic reporter counts down to the weekend for his morning radio audience. Many in his audience are likely thinking all week about the arrival of Saturday and the sweet experience of teeing off in the morning mist.

Paul told Timothy that physical exercise is of "some value" (1 Timothy 4:8). Playing golf can provide regular exercise and recreation that can help restore our perspective, tone up our muscles, and recharge our batteries. But Paul said that "godliness is profitable for all things, having promise of the life that now is and of that which is to come" (v. 8 NKJV).

FAST FACT:
According to the PGA, about 27 million Americans play golf.

The trouble is that many people—Christians included—overdo the golf thing. They emphasize physical exercise almost to the exclusion of spiritual exercise. Paul also said, "Exercise yourself toward godliness" (v. 7 NKJV). Regular spiritual exercise such as prayer, Bible study, walking in the Spirit, sharing Christ with others, serving others, and living a pure and holy life are "profitable" for both time and eternity.

Looking forward to the weekend and a day of chasing golf balls around the links is fine. There's nothing wrong with golfing and other forms of recreation. But remember, the greatest profit comes from exercising "toward godliness."

— DAVE EGNER

PLAYING THROUGH

What is your favorite exercise? Golf? Jogging? Basketball? Lifting weights? Something else? What is your favorite spiritual exercise? Which do you do more often?

From the Guidebook: Read 1 Timothy 4:6–11.

NO. 90: SAGE VALLEY COUNTRY CLUB, GRANITEVILLE, SOUTH CAROLINA

> 7,245 yards; built in 2001
> Architect: Tom Fazio
> Another of the exclusive member-only clubs with just over
> 200 members

91. WATCH AND PRAY

"Be self-controlled and alert. Your enemy the devil prowls around like a roaring lion looking for someone to devour."

1 PETER 5:8–9

Did you ever notice that the devil likes to 1. attack special commitments we have with God, and 2. add roadblocks to situations where we can use our God-given gifts?

According to John MacArthur, this is because Satan "hates the righteous as much as he hates God" and since Jesus chose us "out of the world" (John 15:19), the devil therefore "pursues Christians and sets the whole world in motion against them."

In terms of commitments, Satan attempts to distract me from Scripture reading, prayer time, sexual purity, and taking care of my health (His temple). In regard to roadblocks, Satan loves to fuel negative thinking. I find Satan attacks me most on the golf course because he knows golf is something God wants me to use to spread His Good News.

FAST FACT:

Katherine graduated from Pepperdine University in 2003 with a major in sports administration.

Have you ever heard Satan say, "One time won't matter," "One day off won't hurt," or "Other people do worse things?" In his book, *No Wonder They Call Him the Savior*, Max Lucado writes, "You know your weaknesses. You also know the situations in which your weaknesses are most vulnerable. Stay out of those situations. Whatever it is that gives Satan a foothold in your life, stay away from it." Reading and recalling Scripture and continually praying (1 Thessalonians

5:17) will also help us be more prepared when assaulted by fear and temptation. First Corinthians 16:13 and 2 Corinthians 10:5 are great verses to recite when you feel sabotaged by Satan.

Mark 14:38 says, "Watch and pray so that you will not fall into temptation." Are you praying, guarding your thoughts, and avoiding Satan's lures?

—KATHERINE HULL

PLAYING THROUGH

What commitments is Satan trying to sabotage in your life? What roadblocks is he putting in your way? What is your plan for thwarting him?

From the Guidebook: Read Ephesians 6:10–17.

NO. 91: THE HOMESTEAD, HOT SPRINGS, VIRGINIA; CASCADES COURSE

6,659 yards; built in 1923

Architect: William Flynn

Golfers play with the Allegheny Mountains as their backdrop; host of the 2009 USGA Women's Senior Amateur

92. THE VALUE OF FRIENDS

"If one falls down, his friend can help him up."
ECCLESIASTES 4:10

Although my friends from my pre-LPGA Tour days have scattered, they are still very important to me. Except for the occasional times we're in the same place, we have to deepen our relationships through e-mail, over the phone, or through letters. Fortunately, while on the LPGA Tour I am able to get together with other Christian women—new friends who share my faith. We meet weekly for Bible study, fellowship, and prayer.

FAST FACT:

Tracy had a story published in the book Chicken Soup for the Golfer's Soul.

This was especially meaningful a few years ago when my mother died. I was so grateful for friends who let me go through the grieving process at my own pace and who were there for me when I just needed to cry. They supported me at the funeral and at the height of everything going on. My close friends continue to help me remember the special memories of my mom. They encourage me to stay strong in the Lord and to experience His grace and comfort in difficult times.

My friends helped give me the confidence to get back on the Tour and to believe in my abilities as a golfer again after experiencing the pain of my mother's death.

College friends and my friends on the Tour have walked with me through the hard and fun times in life. But most important, they've helped me grow in my Christian faith. This faith has taught me that my worth is from Jesus—and only Him—not from how I perform on the golf course.

Friends. Faith. What a great combination.

—TRACY HANSON

PLAYING THROUGH

In what way have you been a good friend to someone recently? What does it cost you to give enough of yourself to be a friend?

From the Guidebook: Read 1 Samuel 20.

NO. 92: SEA ISLAND GOLF CLUB, SEA ISLAND, GEORGIA; SEASIDE COURSE

7,005 yards; built in 1919

Architect: Walter Travis

Located at the southern tip of St. Simons Island off the eastern coast of Georgia

www.seaisland.com

93. HELP ME!

*"One of his disciples said to [Jesus],
'Lord, teach us to pray.'"*

LUKE 11:1

Pride—the quick and simple reason so many of us are unwilling to ask for help in so many areas of life.

Yet most of us are exceedingly quick to seek a rescuer when our golf game falls to pieces. If we don't run to our favorite pro, we at least run to our friends—those who are playing well—and say, "I can't figure it out. I'm hitting it everywhere. What am I doing wrong?" We practically *beg* them to teach us.

FAST FACT:
Need help with your golf game? Go to www. wallyarmstrong. com.

Well, here is today's simple lesson: As willing as we are to ask for help with our troubled golf game, that is how willing we must begin to be in asking God to teach us.

The disciple who noticed Jesus praying requested something rare in our conversations with God: instruction. That disciple knew there was a hole in his spiritual discipline, and he asked Jesus to teach him and his friends to pray.

We must follow this disciple's example. We must look at our own lives and find our lack. We must identify the kind of training that would push us forward. Then we must ask God to teach us what we need to know, fully prepared to follow His instruction.

Let's each begin with one matter, one area, one discipline—and learn the joy of the Father's regimen. And from our learning we will learn to ask for more.

—JEFF HOPPER

PLAYING THROUGH

Are you willing to get the training you need to grow in Christ? What areas of discipline do you need to improve on?

From the Guidebook: Read Luke 11.

NO. 93: TREETOPS RESORT, GAYLORD, MICHIGAN, PREMIER COURSE

6,832 yards; built in 1987
Architect: Tom Fazio
Fazio's only Michigan course, located in Northern Lower Michigan; location was originally a ski resort, but golf was added in the late twentieth century
www.treetops.com

94. GOLF'S SOLO ACT

Approach Shot:
Focusing on others' needs

*"Each of you should look not only to your own interests,
but also to the interests of others."*

PHILIPPIANS 2:4

Golf is one of sports' true solo acts. Because it's an individual contest, professional golfers have no teammate to rely on or to blame or praise during their round.

There are no missed blocks in golf, no fumbled passes, dropped batons, or lack of teammate chemistry. Golfers have a caddie to carry their clubs and offer advice or encouragement, but they can't hit any shots for the golfers.

FAST FACT:

Bob Estes, a Texas native, captured his first PGA win in 1994. He also won two tournaments in 2001 and one in 2002.

Whatever a player shoots on the professional Tour during his or her round, that's the score. A golfer has no one to blame or praise but good, old No. 1. Because the game can be so individualistic and so mental, golfers often say they don't know their score at the end of a round.

Christian golfers often struggle to keep their focus on their faith when experiencing rough times on the golf course. In the late 1990s, Bob Estes was going through a particularly rough stretch one fall. He was driving to the course one day when he saw a crippled man sitting by the side of the road.

"It was in that moment I lost my self-pity and my wallowing in my current situation," Estes said. "God had given me the ability and the opportunity to play golf for a living. Seeing him by the side of the road made we realize how fortunate I really was."

Focus is important as we do our jobs, but we have to make sure we aren't so inwardly focused that we don't see the many great opportunities God has provided to serve others.

—ART STRICKLIN

PLAYING THROUGH

Do your problems outweigh your opportunities? Thank God for both and seek to serve others whose problems are more severe than yours.

From the Guidebook: Read the book of Psalms to see how God helped David through his series of tough times.

NO. 94: OCONEE AT REYNOLDS PLANTATION, GREENS-BORO, GEORGIA

7,029 yards; built in 2002

Architect: Rees Jones

Host of 2007 PGA Cup and the 2008 PGA Professional National Championship

www.reynoldsplantation.com

95. GOD KNOWS

Approach Shot:
Trusting God's provision

"Therefore I tell you, do not worry about your life."
MATTHEW 6:25

During the summer of 2003, I had my best season ever on the Futures Golf Tour. I finished eighteenth on the money list, making just over $17,000.

Unfortunately, that was not enough to cover the last big bill I had to pay. In order to enter the LPGA qualifying tournament, I had to pay an entry fee of $3,000. I simply did not have the money. I was challenged to trust God to send me the money if He still wanted me to play golf. I prayed, waited, and trusted.

FAST FACT:
When Kristen was on the Futures Tour, she led the golfers' Bible study.

Two weeks before the deadline, I checked my mail and found a sealed envelope waiting for me. I opened it and inside was a cashier's check for $2,000. The card was not signed, and there was no return address. The only words written were "Dream Big." I was thrilled, elated, but mostly humbled. To this day, I have only one explanation for that check: God knew I needed the money, and He got it to me.

Later on that year, I qualified for the LPGA and enjoyed my rookie season in 2004. I learned once again that God provides. It is that simple. He knows exactly what we need precisely when we need it. Our challenge is to learn to trust God and wait on Him. To often we dart out in front of Him instead of being still and letting God work in His wonderful ways.

God knows what your need is right now. Talk to Him about it, be obedient, and then see what He can do.

—Kristen Samp

PLAYING THROUGH

What needs do you have that can be handed over to God? What are some ways in which you can trust God more instead of worrying?

From the Guidebook: Read Matthew 6:25–34.

NO. 95: BARTON CREEK RESORT, AUSTIN, TEXAS, CANYONS COURSE

7,153 yards; built in 2002

Architect: Tom Fazio

Friendly to the environment, the Canyons Course is certified as an Audubon International Signature Sanctuary.

96. QUALITY TIME

*"Come near to God and he will
come near to you."*

JAMES 4:8

Do you spend as much time reading the Bible and praying as you do watching TV or hanging out with friends? Psalm 1:2 tells us to delight in the law of the Lord and meditate on it "day and night." Are you setting aside quiet time for God every day?

According to Gary Chapman, author of *The Five Love Languages*, God's primary love language is quality time. So what does this mean? This means that God has a personality, and we need to get personal with Him. As Max Lucado put it, this doesn't mean relying on others for daily spiritual experiences. He goes on to say that if we don't let people vacation, eat, or sleep on our behalf, why should we let our spiritual experiences be second-hand? The truth is, Jesus spent a lot of alone time with God, and we need to do the same. We need to "be imitators of God" (Ephesians 5:1).

FAST FACT:
LPGA golfer Katherine Hull was born in Brisbane, Australia.

In order to think and act like Christ Jesus (Philippians 2:5), we need to follow Joshua 1:8 and not let the Book of the Law depart from our mouth. Praying continually (1 Thessalonians 5:17) and taking "captive every thought to make it obedient to Christ" (2 Corinthians 10:5) will also help us stay in the Word.

The formula is simple: Loving God equals seeking God—which leads to knowing God. And that all takes quality time with the Father.

—KATHERINE HULL

PLAYING THROUGH

How would you answer Katherine's question: Do you spend more time watching TV or reading the Bible? What steps should you take toward correcting that?

From the Guidebook: Read James 4.

NO. 96: CARLTON WOODS, THE WOODLANDS, TEXAS; SIGNATURE COURSE

7,368 yards; built in 2000
Architect: Jack Nicklaus
A prestigious club built around a private, gated community
www.carltonwoods.com

97. "FORE" BETTER OR WORSE

*"Husbands, love your wives, just as
Christ loved the church."*

EPHESIANS 5:25

For a long time, a golf course called Meadowlane lay within a chip shot of our backyard. Now it has been replaced by another housing development, but when the course was there I had mixed feelings. I like to golf occasionally, but living so close to a reminder of my failures at the game had its disadvantages. I forgot the good times, and I started to recall only those nightmarish days when I would just as soon throw my whole set of clubs into the water.

FAST FACT:
There are nearly 16,000 golf courses in the United States.

When I stood in my backyard looking at that course, I could see ponds hungrily waiting for my next slice or hook. I could imagine sand traps and trees joking about my bad days.

A similar problem can occur in marriage. Sometimes husbands and wives lose sight of the hopes and dreams they once shared. Then the very presence of the other person becomes a source of irritation, reminding the spouse of past failures and disappointments.

When the apostle Paul wrote his letter to the Christians who lived in Ephesus, Asia Minor (now Turkey), around 60 A.D., he asked husbands and wives to turn their thoughts to their relationship with Jesus Christ (5:22–33). In Him we find undying love and forgiveness for our failures. In Him we find

Someone who loves to forget the worst and bring out the best. In Him we find a reminder not of what we've lost but of what we have yet to find. In Him we find the example of the kind of husband or wife each of us who is married is supposed to be.

—MART DeHaan

PLAYING THROUGH

Make a special effort today to tell your spouse, "I love you," and if necessary, "I forgive you" or "I'm sorry." Then do what you can to make proper communication a habit.

From the Guidebook: Read Matthew 19:1–9.

NO. 97: KARSTEN CREEK, STILLWATER, OKLAHOMA
7,407 yards; built in 1994
Architect: Tom Fazio
Named after Karsten Solheim, the man who started the PING golf club company; the back nine of the course surrounds Lake Louise
www.karstencreek.com

98. POWER TO PERSEVERE

"We considered blessed those who have persevered ."
JAMES 5:11

Professional golfer Paula Creamer had worked all year long to earn a berth in the 2008 ADT Championship, the year's final tournament on the LPGA tour. When the event began, however, Creamer was suffering from peritonitis, a painful inflammation of the abdominal wall. Throughout the four days of the tournament, she was in constant pain and unable to eat. She even spent a night in the hospital because of the condition. Still, she persevered to the end and, amazingly, she finished third. Her determination earned her many new fans.

FAST FACT: *When Paula Creamer was selected to play for the US in the 2011 Solheim Cup.*

The challenges and crises of life can tax us to the very end of our strength, and in such times it is easy to want to give up. But James offers followers of Christ another perspective. He says that while life is a battle, it is also a blessing: "As you know, we considered blessed those who have persevered. You have heard of Job's perseverance and have seen what the Lord finally brought about. The Lord is full of compassion and mercy" (James 5:11).

In Job's example, we find encouragement and the power to persevere in life's darkest hours. The strength that kept Job going despite his setbacks was this: His power rooted in God, who is compassionate and merciful.

Even when life is painful and hard, we can persevere because God is there. His mercy endures forever (Psalm 136).

—Bill Crowder

PLAYING THROUGH

What is your battle right now? Does it often feel as if you would rather give up than keep at it? Why not contemplate the Lord's compassion and mercy, and then ask Him to help you to persevere through your most troubling challenges .

From the Guidebook: Read James 5:1-11.

NO. 98: THE BROADMOOR, COLORADO SPRINGS, COLORADO; MOUNTAIN COURSE

7,637 yards; built in 2006

Architect: Jack Nicklaus

This new Mountain links is a redesign of a course on which Nicklaus won the 1959 US Amateur; the original was built in 1918.

www.broadmoor.com

99. HONESTLY!

"The man of integrity walks securely."
PROVERBS 10:9

Golf is a game of integrity and honor. There are no whistles or line judges. It's up to each player to play by the rules. During the 2000 LPGA Championship, golfers and golf fans alike witnessed an act of integrity and honor by a player who understands the importance of playing fair.

Wendy Ward was in the final pairing with Juli Inkster and was still in contention with nine holes to play. After struggling on hole 11, Wendy was trying to compose herself as she faced a long par putt on 13. She set her putter behind the ball and glanced at the hole. When she looked back at the ball she noticed it had moved. No one saw the ball move, not even Wendy, but she knew it was now in a different position.

Without hesitation, Wendy stepped away, knowing a rule had been broken. Because she had set her putter behind the ball and touched the ground, she would be deemed to have caused the ball to move out of position. The penalty? One stroke. She would now be putting for bogey, and she would fall another shot behind Juli.

Wendy, a fellow follower of Jesus Christ, called the penalty on herself because she believes in the integrity and honor of the rules of golf. And she realizes that her testimony depends

FAST FACT:

Tracy Hanson played college golf at San Jose State University before joining the LPGA Tour in 1995.

on her integrity. She eventually missed a playoff by one stroke and finished third.

Walking in integrity and doing what is right is not always easy, but God says, "The man of integrity walks securely, but he who takes crooked paths will be found out." Are you looking for ways to live honestly as a testimony to God?

—TRACY HANSON

PLAYING THROUGH

Think of a situation where you must choose to walk in integrity and honor. Ask God to give you the wisdom to make the correct choice. Then write a note in your spiritual journal, reminding yourself what the right action would be.

From the Guidebook: Read about some other issues of integrity in Psalm 15:1–5.

NO. 99: BAY HARBOR, BAY HARBOR, MICHIGAN; THE QUARRY COURSE

Built in 1996

Architect: Arthur Hills

Built along the edge of an old stone quarry and finishing on the shores of Lake Michigan, The Quarry is a unique experience.

www.bayharborgolf.com

100. TICKED

"Do not make friends with a hot-tempered man."

PROVERBS 22:24

I like to play golf. I'm terrible at it, but it's fun. Most of the time, anyway. There have been moments when I got so mad at that little white ball that I lost control. I threw things I shouldn't have thrown and said things I shouldn't have said. I was ticked.

It even happens to the best players. A reporter once asked PGA golf pro golfer Craig Stadler why he had a new putter. He said, "Because the last one didn't float too well."

FAST FACT:

The Web site golfwinningtouch. com suggests, "Direct the feeling [of anger] into a resolution for practice. Punish yourself with remedial practice."

Maybe you recall the TV commercial where a guy loses it on the course after a bad shot. He grabs some clubs and flings them into a nearby pond. His rage still wasn't satisfied, so he picks up the whole bag and heaves that into the water. Only then does he realize that it was his friend's bag of clubs that were given a bath. Ooops.

That's what can happen when you get so mad you lose control. Believe me, I know. You probably do too. It can happen with anything you do, not just golf.

We've all felt the pain caused by anger that's out of control. That's why the Bible's words about control are so helpful. It says the Spirit of God can control the response of emotions like anger (Galatians 5:16–21). All we need is the desire to let

Him have control. God alone can calm the rage when we're ticked.

We need the self-control of His Spirit. This will not be easy for us, but it is possible. I find hope in knowing that—especially out on the links.

—DAN DEAL

PLAYING THROUGH

Write down what makes you lose control of your anger. Then read the two Scripture passages in "From the Guidebook." Let it sink in, and jot down how God can help you control the very things that make you mad.

From the Guidebook: Look at Ephesians 4 after you've read Galatians 5. Good stuff!

NO. 100: FALLEN OAK, BILOXI, MISSISSIPPI

7,487 yards; built in 2006

Architect: Tom Fazio

The course meanders through a variety of Southern-style foliage, including pecan and magnolia groves and old-growth oaks.

www.fallenoak.com

KEY VERSE LIST

Verse	Article Number	Title
Exodus 20:3	58	A Slow Fourth
Deuteronomy 8:11	84	Fore!-Getful
Deuteronomy 8:18	57	What to Give God
Joshua 1:7	12	Strong and Courageous
Joshua 1:8	56	The Bible: Our Guide to Life
Joshua 14:11	4	Callaway and Caleb
I Samuel 17:45	6	Third-Graders and Shepherd Boys
Nehemiah 2:17	67	Courage Couched Among Cruelty
Job 31:4	40	Guess Who Is Watching?
Psalm 27:8	11	Spend Time with God
Psalm 31:14	62	A Matter of Trust
Psalm 37:5	55	Who's in Charge Here?
Psalm 73:26	9	Feel Like a Failure?
Psalm 96:2	46	Daily Devotion
Psalm 106:1-2	65	Don't Be Stupid
Psalm 111:1	63	"Good Shot!"
Psalm 116:15	68	Wasn't God Watching?
Psalm 119:23–24	89	Captive Thoughts
Psalm 139:14	69	Imperfect by Design
Proverbs 3:5	54	When We Cannot See
Proverbs 10:9	99	Honestly!
Proverbs 13:20	75	Walk with the Wise
Proverbs 14:29	36	I Hate to Lose
Proverbs 15:23	44	A Timely Word
Proverbs 22:24	100	Ticked
Ecclesiastes 4:10	92	The Value of Friends
Isaiah 64:8	8	Chasing No. 1
Jeremiah 29:11	76	God's Got a Plan
Zechariah 4:6	71	Close Calls
Malachi 3:10	81	Can You Outgive God?
Matthew 5:5	39	Real Power

POWER UP! WRITERS
GOLF PEOPLE

Brief biographical notes about the golf people who contributed articles to Power Up!

AARON BADDELEY Born in New Hampshire but raised for much of his youth in Australia, Baddeley has been a champion in two countries. He first made a splash by winning back-to-back Australian Opens as a teenager. Since he returned to the US, he has won the 2006 Verizon Heritage and the 2007 FBR Open. He and his wife Rochelle live in Scottsdale, Arizona.

BEN CRANE Ben and Heather Crane live in Nashville, but he grew up in Oregon. It was there that his grandfather introduced him to golf when he was just five years old. Among his highlights on the course are his two PGA wins: the 2003 BellSouth Classic and the 2005 US Bank Championship.

TRACY HANSON Thanks to a steady career that began in the early 1990s, Hanson is in the Top 100 of all-time LPGA money-earners. Near the beginning of her career, she traveled overseas to play on the Asian Tour, where she won the 1994 Indonesian Open. Hanson likes to write, and has had her work published in multiple outlets, including *Chicken Soup for the Golfer's Soul*.

KATHERINE HULL Katherine graduated from Pepperdine University in 2003 with a degree in Sports Administration. Like Aaron Baddeley, Katherine grew up in Australia. One of her best years on the LPGA circuit was 2005 when she won more than $200,000—helped along by finishing second at the BMO Financial Group Canadian Women's Open. In 2007, she accompanied Betsy King and others on a missions trip to Rwanda.

BETSY KING One of the most celebrated golfers in LPGA history, King won 34 tournaments, earned more than $7 million, and was inducted into the LPGA Hall of Fame in 1995. She also captained the US Solheim Cup team that defeated the Europeans while playing overseas—the first time a Solheim Cup home team did not win. King has been active in overseas missions, both in Europe and in Africa.

SIEW AI LIM A psychology major at the University of South Carolina, Lim has mastered the mind game of golf to make a career out of it. Her best year was 2004 when she earned $177,000 on the courses of the LPGA. Lim enjoys playing the guitar as a part of the LPGA Bible Fellowship that meets on Wednesdays for the ladies on the Tour.

KRISTEN SAMP After Samp graduated from the University of Missouri in 1996, she joined the Futures Tour, where she displayed her spiritual maturity by heading up the FCA Fellowship for two seasons. She has competed in the LPGA Qualifying Tournament four times in order to retain her LPGA card. Her best round on the LPGA circuit was a 67 in 2007 at the Corona Championship.

WENDY WARD Wendy and her husband Nate Hare don't hang out at the seashore when she's not playing golf. They raise cattle and do other farm-related stuff on their ranch in Washington State. Ward captured her first LPGA title in 1997 when she won the Fieldcrest Cannon Classic. She has been a multiple-year member of the US Solheim Cup team.

DEVOTIONAL WRITERS

Brief biographical notes about the writers whose articles appear in the Power Up! *Links edition. Some of these articles first appeared in* Our Daily Bread, *some appeared in* Power Up!, *and some were written especially for this book.*

JEFF ARNOLD As a Chicago Cubs fan, Jeff Arnold probably doesn't get much support on that subject from his co-workers. Arnold is a writer for ChicagoFootball.com. For *Sports Spectrum*, he wrote articles about pitchers Nate Robertson and Mark Redman in addition to being a regular contributor for the *Power Up!* devotional guide.

DAVE BRANON For 18 years, Dave was managing editor of *Sports Spectrum* magazine. Currently, he is an editor for Discovery House and Our Daily Bread Ministries. He is a regular contributing writer for *Our Daily Bread*. Over the years, he has written a number of sports-related books for a variety of publishers.

DAVE BURNHAM For many years, Dave Burnham has been involved in RBC Ministries as a teacher, a writer, and a board member. A longtime pastor, Burnham also heads up the Burnham Ministries International. While in college at Wheaton, Burnham was a captain of the Thunder football team.

JOSH COOLEY A former writer for the *Baltimore Examiner*, Josh serves as a children's ministry administrator at his church in the Gaithersburg, Maryland, community. Cooley has written many articles for *Sports Spectrum*, including profiles of Scott Sanderson, Charlie Ward, and Brian Roberts.

BILL CROWDER A longtime pastor and a longer-time Los Angeles Angels fan, Crowder oversees the content for the publications of Our Daily Bread Ministries, and he represents the ministry internationally by teaching the Bible conferences overseas. He also writes for *Our Daily Bread* and has written several books published by Discovery House.

DAN DEAL After working as a radio producer and occasional host of *Sports Spectrum* radio at RBC Ministries for several years, Deal left to work on the staff of Ada Bible Church in Ada, Michigan, as director of small group training and resources.

MART DEHAAN Mart is senior content advisor of Our Daily Bread Ministries. His grandfather, Dr. M. R. DeHaan, founded Radio Bible Class (now Our Daily Bread Ministries) in 1938. Mart has written several books, including *Been Thinking About*, a publication of Discovery House.

CHRISTIN DITCHFIELD Christin Ditchfield got her start in writing as a contributor to *Sports Spectrum* magazine. She has gone on to publish dozens of books and begin her own writing-speaking-broadcasting ministry called Take It to Heart. Among her most popular books is *A Family Guide to Narnia*.

DAVE EGNER A longtime editor and writer at RBC Ministries, as well as a popular college professor at Cornerstone University, Egner loves anything outdoors. Golf is on that list of favorites, as is fishing and hunting at his cabin in Michigan's Upper Penninsula.

TOM FELTEN A former *Sports Spectrum* magazine writer and administrator—Tom was manager of *SS* radio and magazine for several years—he now is managing editor of *Our Daily Journey*, one of the devotional guides produced by Our Daily Bread Ministries.

TIM GUSTAFSON When not serving in the US Navy Reserves, Tim is an editor for Our Daily Bread Ministries. He and his wife, Leisa, have eight children, just a few of whom have inherited Tim's love for the Detroit Tigers. Gustafson has served the Navy overseas in Japan and the Philippines.

BRIAN HETTINGA The host and producer of the weekly radio program *Discover the Word,* an outreach of Our Daily Bread Ministries, Hettinga played small college basketball before trading in his Chuck Taylors for a microphone. In 2008, he and his sons, Tim and Josh, were on hand at Wrigley Field when the Cubs clinched the National League Central title.

JEFF HOPPER When the question is golf and the Christians who are involved in that sport on a professional level, Jeff Hopper is the man with the answers. He is the editor of *Links Letter,* a publication that tells the stories of the top Christians in both the PGA and the LPGA.

DAVID McCASLAND Known as a consummate biographer, McCasland's most important work was his biography of 1924 Olympic champion and Chinese missionary Eric Liddell. McCasland's book *Pure Gold* goes beyond the *Chariots of Fire* story to tell the real-life version of the life of this man of God. McCasland also writes for the devotional *Our Daily Bread.*

GEORGE McGOVERN McGovern has had the unique opportunity of being the chaplain for championship teams in two different sports: baseball and football. He has been the chaplain for the New York Yankees and the New York Giants for many years.

ANDREW PROVENCE Provence knows sports on the inside. He was a member of the Atlanta Falcons for five seasons in the 1980s. He played in 69 games on the defensive line for the Falcons after a college career at the University of South Carolina.

MOLLY RAMSEYER As a college student, Molly worked with *Sports Spectrum* magazine as an intern. She did such a good job she was offered the chance to write for the magazine later. After college, she began working with Youth for Christ on the local level. Currently, she is national director of camping for Youth for Christ. She lives in Englewood, Colorado, with her husband, Dave.

FRANK REICH While the Buffalo Bills were going to four straight Super Bowls back in the 1980s, Frank Reich was there as Jim Kelly's backup quarterback. But his biggest football claim to fame came when he orchestrated the two biggest comebacks in football history—one while at the University of Maryland and one while with the Bills.

ROXANNE ROBBINS After hobnobbing with the influential and famous in Washington D. C. for several years in positions relating to public relations, Roxanne left it all behind to go to Uganda to live among kids with nothing. A longtime writer for *Sports Spectrum,* she knows athletes up-close and personal, but she has discovered the importance of the oft-neglected little guys and girls who cherish someone who cares for them.

DAVID ROPER A prolific writer, Roper has written several books for men—urging them to live for God—including *A Man to Match the Mountain* and *The Strength of a Man* for Discovery House. He and his wife live in Idaho, which offers him a great opportunity to engage in his favorite recreation: fly-fishing.

ART STRICKLIN Art Stricklin knows golf. He has played many of the top golf courses in America as he has covered the game for *Sports Spectrum,* for *Sports Illustrated,* and for numerous other publications. He and his family live in the Dallas, Texas, area, where he works for Marketplace Ministries, an organization that supplies chaplains for companies all across the United States.

HERB VANDERLUGT For a long time, Herb was one of the most popular writers at RBC Ministries. His clear understanding of theology and life helped him as he wrote for *Our Daily Bread* and for several Discovery Series booklets. A pastor and an avid baseball fan, Herb loved to regale his listeners with stories of his youth as a catcher and as a fan who loved going to Tiger Stadium to see greats like Hank Greenberg play. He continued to work at RBC until his death in 2006.

JOANIE YODER A popular writer for *Our Daily Bread* and for Discovery House Publishers, Joanie lived in England. She and her husband had established a rehabilitation center for drug addicts before she began writing for RBC Ministries. One hundred of her devotionals are collected in the book *God Alone*, available from Discovery House. Yoder died in 2004.

NOTE TO THE READER